Hidden

and

the Royal Gift

Non-Fiction

A story of Survival and a Recovery after living through unimaginable horrors.

Thomas Goldstein

Edited by Joseph Goldstein

For comments or sugestions contact the author at:

HiddenMemoirandtheRoyalGift@gmail.com.

Sales and distribution:

Amazon.com

ISBN : 9798324261108

<u>Book Front Cover Explained</u>

The narrative of "The Hidden Memoir and the Royal Gift" unfolds through the lives of four women show-cased on the book front cover: My mother, Bracha, the author of the memoir, along with her sister Miriam, and her husband's sisters Rivka and Esther.

In the heart of the cover lies an oval image depicting the harrowing "Selection" of Hungarian Jews on the ramp at <u>Auschwitz-II-Birkenau</u>   during the Holocaust's final phase in 1944. Jews were sent either to work or to the gas chamber[1].

Above, an oval picture adorned with a rising sun symbolizes the profound hope bestowed by the Danish and

---

[1] This momentous photograph, is part of the collection known as the <u>Auschwitz Album</u>,
(<u>https://en.wikipedia.org/wiki/Auschwitz_Album</u>) which was donated to Yad Vashem by Lili Jacob, a survivor, who found it in the <u>Mittelbau-Dora concentration camp</u> (<u>https://en.wikipedia.org/wiki/Mittelbau-Dora_concentration_camp</u>) in 1945. The Auschwitz Album is the only surviving visual evidence of the mass atrocities perpetrated at Auschwitz-Birkenau.

Swedish people, and the royal gift. This gift came across the sea, from his Magesty - The King of Sweden.

<u>Dedication</u>

To the loving memory of my dear parents, Bracha and Tzvi, and to Bracha's sister Miriam, along with Tzvi's sisters Esther and Rivka whose resilience and bravery in the face of the Holocaust allowed them to rebuild their shattered world.

To the the loving memory of Itzchak and Henye Pollak (Parents of Thomas Goldstein's wife) who as a maried couple also survived the Holocaust and were succesful in reconstructing their destroyed world.

Additionally, in loving memory of Chaya Goldstein (the beloved wife of Joseph Goldstein) and to our cherished cousins Sara (Ella) Haham and Tzvia (Elaine-Lonci) Zicherman, whose prematurely departure left an irreplaceable void in our lives.

This book is also dedicated to the compasionate people of Sweden, and to their honorable king, whose assitance to my mother and many of the other surviving victims, restored their dignity and humanity in the aftermath of World War II.

Hidden Memoir and the Royal Gift

The purpose of this book

This book recounts the Holocaust survival story of my mother, Barbara (known as Bracha in Hebrew and Boris in Hungarian), her sister, Manci (Miriam in Hebrew), and her husband's two sisters, Esther, and Regina (Rivka in Hebrew).

Based on a memoir penned by my mother immediately after her liberation from the German death camps, this book preserves the original account, and it is a historical document stored in Yad Vashem[2]. Bracha's memoir serves as an eyewitness testimony to the persecution and murder of innocent Jewish civilians, who had committed no crimes, and posed no threat to anyone. Nonetheless, they were subjected to persecution, torture, enslavement, and murder solely because they were born to Jewish parents.

The narrative within this book vividly brings history to life, reminding us to transcend the anonymous, impersonal statistics of the past. It prompts us to remember the Jewish men, women, and children who were persecuted, imprisoned, tortured, and murdered by the Germans during the Holocaust.

In tribute to their memory, this publication primarily utilizes their Hebrew names.

---

[2] Yad Vashem is the World Holocaust Remembrance Center in Jerusalem, Israel.

Additionally, this book narrates the uplifting account of how the people of Denmark and Sweden assisted my mother in reclaiming her humanity, and how the King of Sweden facilitated her reunion with her beloved husband in her native country of Romania.

Furthermore, this book features original poems composed by Holocaust survivors. Poetry emerged as a powerful medium for expressing their emotions, pain, and suffering, as well as their longing for freedom.

Table of Contents

Prologue

My name is Thomas Goldstein, and I was born to save my mother's life.

In most cases, the birth of a newborn endangers a mother's life; but, in my case, it was exactly the opposite. My arrival was a necessity to prevent my mother, Bracha, from succumbing to despair and contemplating suicide. After her horrific Holocaust experiences, where her children, parents, brothers, and sisters had all been brutally murdered by the Germans, my mother, broken in body and mind, but miraculously still alive, returned to her native town in Romania.

Equally miraculously, she was reunited there with her husband, (my father Tzvi) who, against all odds, also survived the Holocaust. Together, they found that their village had been utterly devastated. Every broken street, house, and tree served as a painful reminder of a loved one lost during the Holocaust. The weight of survivor's guilt and depression grew so heavy that my mother found herself contemplating suicide, often walking along the nearby train tracks.

Fortunately, in her hometown lived a very compassionate and understanding doctor who tried to help her. This doctor suggested that one way for her to regain her sanity would be to summon the courage to start a family anew, to have a child, and embark on a new life with a fresh sense of purpose.

That is why I was brought into the world - to give my mother that new sense of purpose and a new lease on life.

I am told that her transformation was nothing short of miraculous. My mother, somehow, succeeded in moving beyond her painful memories of the past. She started a new life, full of hope, and an unquenchable determination to provide a brighter future for her new family. Soon after, my brother Joseph joined our family, further affirmation of my mother's courage and belief in the possibility of a better future.

My mother never talked to us about her Holocaust experiences. Her conversations with her children and grandchildren always revolved around happy and beautiful experiences. She created a safe, imaginary world for us, one filled with beautiful stories and uplifting anecdotes.

I will always remember my mother as a very optimistic and happy person, who had a beautiful voice and often sang to us. She enjoyed celebrating happy events like birthdays, anniversaries, and graduations. Growing up, we remained blissfully unaware of her pain and nightmares, as she buried them deep within her memory trying to ensure our safety and happiness.

Now, as I am reading and translating her incredible memoir, I am stunned and shaken by the immense humiliation, pain, and horror she endured during the Holocaust. It remains incomprehensible to me that after enduring the horrors of German death camps and losing her beautiful two children, brothers, sisters, and parents, she somehow managed to rebuild a normal life filled with love, hope, and optimism.

Astonishingly, she never lost her faith or her belief in a brighter future. I am convinced that writing her memoir was a vital step in her healing process, allowing her to begin laying her nightmares to rest. When my brother and I were born she invested all her energies and aspirations into our futures.

While growing up, we knew that she was taken to the concentration camps by the Germans, but never knew any of the details of her tragedy. Occasionally we saw her crying over some old pictures, but she wiped away her tears, and put on a happy face, soon as she saw her children watching her. These horrific details were only revealed to us after discovering her memoir. This memoir, written in Hungarian[3] right after her liberation, detailed the many terrible and nightmarish events she had experienced during the Holocaust. This document was hidden in her Brooklyn apartment, and we only found it after she became sick and moved out.

At the time, we immediately recognized the significance and importance of this original document. My brother Joseph, arranged to have the original document donated to Yad Vashem[4], to be preserved in a controlled environment, as an invaluable historic document.[5]

I had a strong desire to ask my mother questions, but due to her illness, I chose to withhold my inquiries. Later, I recognized that she hid her memoir because she was trying to bury her painful past. Asking questions would have only resurrected her painful memories. I did manage to get some answers to my questions from friends and family members who survived the horrors of the Holocaust with her.

With the assistance of my two Israeli cousins, Ana, and Ella (Miriam's daughters), the original memoir was translated earlier from Hungarian into Hebrew, and from Hebrew into

---

[3] See Appendix A – first page of Bracha's original Memoir.
[4] Yad Vashem is the World Holocaust Remembrance Center in Jerusalem, Israel.
[5] See Appendix A for the actual document reference number.

English, by the Sarah Yad Foundation's Life Stories Project.

In this new rendition, I decided to translate my mother's original Hungarian memoir directly into English. This new rendition includes maps, pictures, and historical references, to help explain and clarify her story. Throughout the book, the translation of my mother's *original memoir appears in purple italics,* to distinguish it from the commentaries and rest of the text.

My intent is to document the courage and faith displayed by my mother during and after her terrifying, unimaginable experiences. I hope readers will focus not only on the horrifying facts of the Holocaust but also appreciate my mother's strength and courage in helping her sister and many other young women to survive the Nazi horrors.

I also hope readers will acknowledge the compassionate care and affection shown by the Danish and Swedish people to the Holocaust survivors. My mother's memoir is full of praises and blessings for the Danish and the noble Swedish people. They were the ones who helped restore her humanity and identity with a name, rather than a disposable slave laborer with a number tattooed on her arm.

Very notably and memorably, the King of Sweden recognized her as a valuable human being and helped her return to her hometown in Romania, with a gift for her reunion with her husband[6].

---

[6] See Chapter 4- Rest of Bracha's Story

<u>Chapter 1 - The Start of Bracha's Memoir</u>

The tragic life of an unhappy mother – during the years, 1944-45.

This memoir was written by my mother on *June 29th, 1945, in the Pulmonary Sanatorium, Landskona, Sweden.*

I am at the bedside of my beloved young sister. The recent memories that come to my mind are very painfully sad. I shall try to recount the events of our terrible tragedy.

Up until 1943, my dear husband and I were leading a very happy life until he was conscripted to the labor camp in Baia Mare (Nagy Bánya – in Hungarian).

This forced deportation, at gunpoint, of all able-bodied Jewish males was an integral nefarious element in the malevolent fascist Hungarian regime's plan. Separating all able-bodied Jewish men from their families and forcing them into slave labor camps, effectively left their families unprotected. The remaining defenseless Jews found themselves at the mercy of the cruel, antisemitic, fascist rulers.

I was living very happily in Valea lui Mihai (Romania) *and I was very content with my small home. We had two handsome, healthy sons. The elder one was 8 years old, named Pityuka, and the younger one was 6 years old, named Tibike. As long as my husband was with us, our days were full of joy. When he was taken away, everything collapsed. That is when the tragedy of my life began.*

The Hungarian government joined the German Nazis in World War II and produced an evil plan for the Jewish population under their control.   They force able-bodied Jewish men to work in brutal slave labor brigades on the most dangerous jobs. They were thus able to utilize these helpless victims in the dangerous labor camps,[7] and leave the remaining Jewish population unprotected and impoverished.   During   those   times,   men   were predominantly the breadwinners, and families relied on a single source of income.

My parents lived in a farming community where their income came mostly from my father's book binding job. He also delivered newspapers for his father's small store that sold mostly books, newspapers, tobacco, and other candy-store like products.

However, with the absence of husbands and their income, families were compelled to deplete their scant resources to provide sustenance for their children, who frequently went to bed hungry.

---

[7] See - References – Sources of Knowledge
       Satellite picture of the road built by the Jewish
       Slave Laborers

Our Happy Family was Uprooted by the Germans –

Beginning of our Terrible, Endless Agony

Bracha and Tzvi with their two sons before being caught up in the horrible events of the Holocaust.

March 1944 was the start of Spring, which also brought with it great misery – terrible, endless agony. On March 19th the news spread like lightning. The SS German soldiers, who were the horror of Europe, had occupied Hungary. Our normal life was disrupted overnight. Total chaos prevailed everywhere – logic had come to an end. Everyone, and especially we Jews, wept in grief and we kept asking ourselves what should we do? We prayed to God – what would our fate be? Dear God, we beseech you to protect us, to save us from the decrees the Germans had imposed upon the Jews in Poland, Slovakia, and other small countries they had invaded so ruthlessly.

Yes, indeed, the sad truth was a reality. The skies above us darkened and the storm was approaching rapidly – the storm that uprooted so many family trees, with many thousands of dead victims. The Hungarian media, radio, and newspapers were filled with obscene Jewish hatred.

The very efficient and effective German/Hungarian propaganda machine was able to disseminate obscene lies and disinformation. These lies and disinformation could not be contested because the Germans controlled all means of communication (newspapers, magazines, radios). They also passed laws that would make it illegal to oppose their propaganda machine. Their aim was to dehumanize the Jewish population.

The first decree, issued on April 5th,1944 was the "yellow star." Every Jew aged 6 to 70 years was obliged to wear the yellow star on the left side of the upper item of clothing. As of April 6th, one could distinguish this humiliating patch from a distance. The brighter it shone, the more our future darkened.

I cannot remember the exact date, perhaps it was April 8th, when a new law was issued. Huge posters appeared on the walls prohibiting the use of any vehicle by Jews.

Because of this prohibition, Jews were unable to use any trains, busses, cars, or any means of transportation, to try and escape the rapidly approaching disaster. Confined to a very small area, local Jewish communities were trapped, making it easy for enthusiastic, local Hungarian police to capture them and force them into ghettos.

A new decree appeared every day. Jews were forbidden, under threat of arrest, to leave their homes. Those arrested were tortured in a way that cannot be described. The prisons and detention centers were packed with innocent people. A star sewn loosely to the outer article of clothing was enough to deliver a person into the hands of those cruel murderers.

In the middle of April huge placards proclaimed the immediate closing down of all Jewish shops. The owners were ordered to hand over all their property and jewelry. Very eagerly, the Germans immediately implemented all these laws.

During this period, Jewish people were cruelly deprived of their humanity and denied fundamental human rights. They endured degradation, physical assaults, and violence without any repercussions. Seeking assistance from the authorities or expecting protection was a futile endeavor.

Under the Hungarian Fascist laws, the killing of a Jewish person did not qualify as murder. This reprehensible policy encouraged local Hungarians to actively participate in identifying and rounding up Jewish individuals. Subsequently they forced them into ghettos and robbed them of their belongings.

Everyone was in deep despair. My beloved parents and my siblings, dearer to me than my life, were in the same town. My mother cried in endless misery, knowing how dark the future of her children loomed, especially when the expulsion of the Jews from the county of Maramureş[8] began.

---

[8] Maramureş is a geographical, historical, and cultural region in northern Romania and western Ukraine. It is situated on the northeastern Carpathian Mountains, along the upper Tisza River.

Gathering Jews into Overcrowded Ghettos

At that time, we did not yet know the word "ghetto" or what it meant. Freight trains kept arriving day and night packed with our tormented Jewish brothers. "Where to?" we asked ourselves. Only later did we know the answer.

There was great confusion in Valea lui Mihai. We sneaked around in fear and ran in crowds to the railway station when the arrival of a train was signaled. Everyone was carrying baskets full of food to help our poor brothers. The cruel gendarmes were equipped with bayonets and looked on with satanic smiles, complacent at the misery of the victims who kept arriving.

Bracha's parents Shaindy and Avigdor Bauer.

This picture may have been taken at some celebration before the holocaust.

They were both murdered by the Nazi criminals.

Valea lui Mihai, Romania my mother's native town, served as a significant border railroad hub where trains made brief stops to replenish steam locomotives with water and coal. The local community witnessed the arrival of trains carrying Jewish individuals in cattle cars, originating from the eastern regions of Hungary, in route to undisclosed destinations.

They dispersed the crowds with the butts of their rifles and with rubber truncheons. Finally, everyone returned home with tearing eyes and trembling knees. The train disappeared with the victims. Later, we heard that they were brought to Mátészalka, to an empty deserted open field in the middle of nowhere.

Mátészalka, located not far from Satu Mare (Szatmár), had been established by the German occupiers and their Hungarian collaborators as a conveniently located ghetto for confining the Jews.

We cried to Heaven and foresaw the same fate befalling us. We felt that cruel fortune would not spare us. The synagogues were filled with ardent prayers. We took upon ourselves vows of fasting that even children, the old, and the sick tried to keep. To our dismay, our prayers were not answered.

Hitler's commands knew no mercy. The local police in Valea lui Mihai had never been as busy as in those days. Every morning brought forth new decrees. Brokenheartedly, we saw the lawyers being marched in the middle of the road by the gendarmes with their bayonets, and later the doctors, and still later the real estate owners, and ultimately no one was safe from the claws of the Gestapo.

In their characteristic fashion, the Germans devised a highly systematic plan for the destruction of the Jewish communities. Initially, they apprehended all the leaders, including the most prominent and affluent Jews. This strategy enabled them to plunder significant Jewish assets while eliminating the potential for any remaining leadership capable of organizing resistance against their heinous actions.

Bracha's husband Tzvi in the Hungarian forced labor camp, 1942.

Notice the band on his left arm. It displayed the yellow star of David indicating that he was Jewish.

Tzvi was lucky to have been in a forced labor camp that was headed by a more humane officer.
In this camp they worked him extremely hard, but they seem to have provided him the ability to take a picture and send letters to his beloved wife and family.

We all shared the same fate. My poor husband felt from afar that a terrible disaster was raging. Every day a letter arrived full of despair. In the last letter he said farewell to me.

I was no longer the woman I had been. My home was in total disorder, but I was utterly indifferent. I was fearfully listening to every voice.

God, what will our fate be? We were told that we would be taken to the ghetto in Oradea (Nagyvárad in Hungarian). Fear prevailed everywhere in town. I wandered about lifelessly, not knowing what would happen to me. My nights were sleepless. I took my husband's letters and read them tearfully. I then tore them up and burnt them so that my husband's loving memories should not fall into the wrong hands.

The days passed and then my beloved elderly parents were also taken by the gendarmes with their bayonets to our synagogue. As I am writing these words, my hand grips my pen helplessly, my eyes are tearing, and I feel I cannot go on.

I continue to be amazed that my mother found the inner strength to write this memoir just a short time after surviving the Holocaust. Most survivors were so traumatized, that for 25 years there were very few first-hand accounts and publications describing the horrors of the Holocaust.

Being Forced into a Ghetto in the City of Oradea[9]

The following day my elder sister, Sarika, her husband and their three handsome boys were taken from their home. That very day, the cruel murderers took out my elder sister, Irenka, and her two beautiful daughters from their home.

*My parents and sisters had been in an overcrowded place for three days without any beds, waiting for us. I was still at home, packed and ready. My turn came only later. My father-in-law (**Yehuda Leib**) and my husband's younger sisters, Esther, and Rivka were with me all that time.*

---

[9] The **Oradea ghetto** was one of the Nazi-era ghettos for European Jews during World War II

Oradea ghetto - Wikipedia	https://en.wikipedia.org/wiki/Oradea_ghetto

BAUER IRENKE - VALEA-LUI MIHAI

Irenke - Bracha's oldest sister

Sarika - Bracha's second-older sister

That awful day, when we were finally ordered to leave our home, arrived.

A cart stopped in front of our home, while my beloved children were playing not suspecting anything. A policeman with two armed gendarmes stopped at our front door and forced me out brutally. An order is an order, and we were obliged to go. We put our baggage on the cart. My two small boys each took their backpacks, everything else was left behind, and we started walking. My cherished possession from my dear husband, my wedding band, which I considered holy, was forcefully ripped off my finger.

My poor father-in-law and his daughters Esther and Rivka left the house in tears. Though we did not know what was awaiting us, we were gripped by a terrible heartache. We were forced, by the police holding rifles with attached bayonets, to parade on the main street until we also reached the Synagogue. My poor parents wept when they saw us.

On that day, the Hungarian gendarmes searched all the women to make sure that they were not hiding any jewelry inside their bodies. We too had to undergo this brutal and humiliating body search. Even on that day, with our bundles on our backs, we stood in groups of one hundred and set out on the sorrowful march to the railway station. A freight train was already waiting for the victims. This is how we arrived in the city of Oradea.

Overcrowded in an Open Sky Ghetto

Our so-called apartment turned out to be a storehouse for junk wood, without a door, without any walls and without a ceiling. Full of fear, we concluded that we were practically homeless on the street.

May 1st - all the Jews of the town were already in the ghetto. The wealthy Jews had been tortured before they were thrown into the ghetto, accused that they had not handed over all their property (gold, silver, jewelry) to the authorities. The ghetto was overcrowded. In the courtyard, the healthy, beautiful, and innocent children were humming like bees in a nest. The sight was terrifying, but even the youngest child was suffering silently, for we thought it would end quickly.

But the Germans were dissatisfied with the fact that 15,000 people were crowded together. Then came a new order; all the Jews from the surrounding area were to be brought together in this Oradea ghetto.

Tears, despair, and questions – dear God, how will all these people be crowded in? There was no space to breathe. But the murderers knew no pity.

Towards morning we already heard the rumbling of carts. Desperate fathers, tearful, red-eyed mothers were trying to calm the terrified children, but the escorting gendarmes were shouting brutally and laughing maliciously. They had arrived from the villages. They were not allowed to bring anything except the clothes they were wearing and two days of provisions.

We thought it was the worst sight, but unfortunately, the tragedy was only beginning. Life in the ghetto was terrible. We remained there and suffered, crammed under an open sky, for two weeks.

They Are Packing Us in a Cattle Train

After two weeks, at five in the morning, there was a terrible clamor. Loud voices were hollering that everyone should line up in the yard, which was full of armed gendarmes, pointing their bayonets at the miserable crowd. We heard a loud order to take only one small bag and go in the middle of the yard immediately. Anyone who did not obey the order would be shot on the spot.

The panic was terrible. Fathers and mothers were running around crying bitterly; indeed, a terrible spectacle. We were paralyzed with fear. Me and my sister Irenke, who was with me at this time, had to wake up our innocent children, who had done nothing wrong, from their deep sleep. Our dear tiny ones, who did not suspect anything, were crying bitterly because they had been woken up in panic and wanted to go on sleeping. With fearful and painful hearts, we had to dress our precious little children.

It was raining ruthlessly when we arrived for the lineup. My dear, kind parents and my elder sister, Sarika, were standing ready in a group of 75 people, flanked by the gendarmes with bayonets. I begged desperately to be allowed to join my parents, but the cruel murderers would not listen to me. My beloved mother was terribly pale with her face broken with pain. I saw her begging to let me join them. In response, they whipped her with a rubber truncheon.

With tearing eyes and a broken heart, I had to witness how they left with a group of 75 people. I could not even say goodbye to my dearly beloved parents and my sisters. I could not kiss their hands and thank them for the last time for all they had done for me in the past. They left, and that was the last time I saw my beloved mother, father, sister, and her wonderful children.

And then our turn arrived. A frightful scene – little children in the arms of their mothers, sick and old people who remained last. Numerous sick people who could not walk remained behind, and those murderers beat them to death on the spot.

In the end, after cruel thrashings, we too reached the train station. My poor children could hardly walk in the terrible rain. A long freight train was waiting for the victims, its doors secured with iron locks. A Gestapo sentry marked the door with a large number 75 in white chalk. We realized then that we were in the hands of the Germans. My dear parents were already locked in the wagons. I never saw them again.

We were also chased into a wagon on the train. There were 75 of us – children and old people who were mostly sick. In one of the corners there were 35 loaves of bread and 7 liters of water – the three-day supply for 75 people. We were all brutally pushed in, one on top of each other, counted and locked behind an iron door.

The Germans dehumanized them, compelling them into overcrowded cattle cars with no access to basic necessities such as: food, water, and bathroom facilities.

Then we heard the iron lock being secured. There were two tiny windows in the wagon. One was barbed wire and the other had wooden beams. There were no seats and we each sat on our small bundle.

Where is this train taking us?

The long cattle train started moving. There was an outburst of loud crying. Dear God, where are they taking us? The suffocating heat was unbearable. The little water we had was soon gone. The children were begging for water. There was none. We, the unfortunate mothers, prayed to God for rain, so our children should have water.

Thus, we traveled for three days and three nights, without air and without water. No one could touch the bread as the heat was terrible and the thirst unbearable. My two dear children were clinging to me bravely. The younger children were weeping helplessly all the time... water...water... but there was no water.

We, the mothers, kept on praying for rain, so there should be water for the children. This went on for three days and three nights – no air, no water. No one even touched the bread as the heat was intolerable and the thirst was agonizing. My beloved two children were clinging to me, bearing the suffering bravely.

The younger children were howling all the time .... water...water... With tearing eyes, I looked out through the barbed wire on the windows and begged the Hungarian gendarmes for a little water. But they were merciless. They asked me roughly: "How many dead do you already have?" They threatened to shoot me if I didn't take my head in.

I cannot describe the terror of our journey. Finally, the train stopped at Kasha[10]. We thought we had arrived at our destination, and we could get water for our children; but to our dismay, it was not so. Our disappointment was terrible. The door was opened, and a rough voice called out: "Since you are being transferred to the Germans, who will take everything away from you in any case, you had better hand over your money and all your belongings to us."

We shuddered when we heard this. It meant we were already in the hands of the Gestapo. Where are they taking us? As of that moment, the wheels of the train were replying: "to your death... to your death". We were traveling towards our end.

---

[10] Kasha- is the city of Kosice in Slovakia – See the Map 1

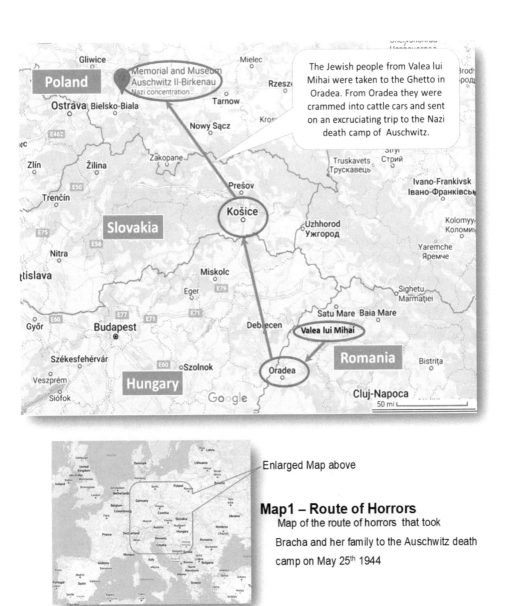

The Jewish people from Valea lui Mihai were taken to the Ghetto in Oradea. From Oradea they were crammed into cattle cars and sent on an excruciating trip to the Nazi death camp of Auschwitz.

Enlarged Map above

Map1 – Route of Horrors

Map of the route of horrors that took Bracha and her family to the Auschwitz death camp on May 25th 1944

Map1 – Route of Horrors

Chapter 2 - Final Destination – Auschwitz - Death Camps

We arrived in Auschwitz on May 25th ,1944.

I had never heard of this place before and I didn't know such atrocities could exist. This was the most tragic day in my life. It was the beginning of a period of horrible events, which I shall be mourning for the rest of my life.

In the morning, the locks were removed from the cattle cars, and the doors opened. A terrible sight was revealed: abandoned parcels, prayer shawls, phylactery, prayer books, documents, souvenirs, a cart harnessed not to horses but to gaunt, emaciated people, who were dragging it. They were dressed in striped clothes and were picking up heavy bundles. A second cart was drawn by young men, instead of horses, and were removing the heavy luggage. The noise was terrible – howling and weeping all around. Then came the striped Polish Jews in striped pajamas who shouted: "Get down quickly and leave everything!"

My poor father-in-law, **(Yehuda Leib)** *who did not sleep for three nights, had neither eaten nor drunk anything, left all his belongings and with tearing eyes and a broken heart took only his prayer shawl bag with phylacteries.*

My grandfather Yehuda-Leib defied the Nazi command and took his tallis and tefillin bag[11] with him as he exited the cattle car. He probably clenched on his sacred possession as he was sent to the gas chamber.

*He got off first, followed by my sisters-in-laws (*Esther, Rivka)*, my two sons and myself. My dear children were holding my hand and clinging to me, as though they felt that this was their last moment with their mother. Thus, hand in hand, we got off the train amongst a mass of people. I searched for my parents but could not see them in the crowd. It was as if the crowd of mourners had swallowed them.*

We walked a few steps and then a German soldier came and dragged my father-in-law away. Then came another killer and tore away my two beautiful sons, whom I had been protecting all my life. He brutally pushed me aside and said that "young mothers will go to work".

I screamed in vain. They had no mercy. I was told that I would see them in another ten minutes. I lost my wits when I realized that I would not be able to remain with my children. I could not even kiss them. They had been taken away, and I was pushed to the right. I only heard the voices

---

[11] His prayer shawl and his phylacteries bag

of my Pityuka and Tibike [12] calling out of the crowd: "Mommy... mommy"... The children and the old people were taken away in a black truck. At that time, we did not yet understand what the black truck meant.

A long line of people started moving in rows of five, counted by the German soldiers. As of that moment, **we were merely numbers**, and every count had to be accurate. We were escorted by the German SS soldiers. There was a terrible noise, out of which you could only hear the muffled sound of crying. Then again, I could only hear "Mommy, Mommy ... Mommy" ... the last calls of my children. Two young women took me by the arms. I was unconscious. Then I grasped the worst of all – that I was no longer holding the hands of my sons, but others were carrying me. I was being dragged away after the murderers tore away my beloved parents, my sisters, and my children.

We begged and cried, but the killers had no mercy[13].

We, the younger people, were taken to the right, to a labor camp. The older people, the children and the sick were taken to the left in the black vehicle. We later knew that those removed to the left were taken straight to the gas chamber or to the crematorium where their bodies were burned. The pen in my hand trembles as I am writing

---

[12] These were Bracha's two beautiful sons. The 8-year-old Pityuka and the 6-year-old Tibike.

[13] I often wondered, what if my two brothers miraculously survived? Many times, I dreamt that I actually met them on the street and somehow, I found out that they were my brothers, and I was able to reconnect with them.
What an impossible dream that was.

these lines, knowing that I must write such woeful truths about my dear family.

Horrible Sights – Smell of Burned Bodies All Over the Camp

The sight was horrible. The whole camp was burning red from the flames that we saw burning day and night. The wind was spreading the terrible odor of the smoke that was rising from the burnt bodies. We knew that the souls of our beloved family were mingled in that smoke. Those sights and days were the worst of my life.

We were taken to a camp to get washed – a huge camp with electrified barbed wire. A huge white sign with a gigantic skull was posted every meter. We passed through the gate and entered a large hall in which SS German soldiers with large rubber clubs were waiting for us. The whole mass of people was driven into the hall where the soldiers made us stand.

A Slovakian girl who spoke Hungarian got up on a chair and said: "Girls, now you are here. We arrived here three years ago, and we went through all that you are going through now. Get undressed; don't bring anything with you; you are going to wash." The girls looked at each other, whispered and cried: Oh God! How can we get undressed? The hall is full of men!

We suppressed our weeping and stood there stark naked. The soldiers made us stand in lines and, still naked, we entered another hall in which men and women were standing together. The girls' beautiful braids were sheared off abruptly and all hair was removed, making them bald. I also went through that, of course. After being shaved, we were taken into another hall with no windows or doors. A strong wind was blowing on our wet bodies from all over the place.

Men and women were waiting for us here as well. Our shaved heads were dipped in a scorching lotion that caused tremendous burning pain. Our eyes were filled with this so-called disinfectant. The soldiers were yelling all the time "Schnell, schnell!" **(Faster, Faster!)**, *brandishing their lashes at the screaming crowds all the time. Finally, we were given clothes – a short-sleeved summer garment that was already full of lice. We put them on in despair, knowing that we would never get our own clothes back.*

Again, the SS soldiers made us stay in rows of five. A Slovakian girl came along with a pail full of red paint and drew a huge cross on our backs. Again, we stood up in rows under an open sky. There was cold spring rain coming down on us. We stood there for hours bald, famished, barefooted and with our broken spirit. We did not recognize each other; we all looked different and distorted.

Finally, when the only garment on our skin was soaked through, we started walking. Our teeth were chattering with the cold. Heartbroken, we said to ourselves that we could not even save one picture of our beloved family. Everything remained there, and the lice were already chewing at our flesh.

The mournful march started. We looked at each other sorrowfully. Dear God, where were the beautiful young women with their gorgeous hair who had arrived here in this horrible place? We all looked like lunatics, bald, ugly. One girl's garment reached down to the ground, another, up to her knees. Some of them wrapped their heads in rags. You could not tell one from the other.

In the end we were put into some sort of "apartment". The whole area was surrounded by a high-voltage electrified fence, with a very small passageway. There were wooden huts at an equal distance of about a meter on both sides of the railing. We looked at each other as though asking: "Oh God, how will there be enough room for us all in this small area?" We found out very soon that 3,300 young girls could be packed into this small area by those murderers.

14

Women imprisoned in the barracks at Auschwitz.

14 Wikipedia
Women imprisoned in the barracks at Auschwitz
https://www.bing.com/search?q=Women+imprisoned+in+the+barracks+at+Auschwitz+.&qs=n&form=QBRE&sp=-1&lq=0&pq=women+imprisoned+in+the+barracks+at+auschwitz+.&sc=0-47&sk=&cvid=CBE252C3C65D443F864325C01B919B78&ghsh=0&ghacc=0&ghpl=

They were waiting for us, the miserable victims, with huge rubber truncheons in their hands, a gun at their sides, skull and crossbones on their hats, two large SS insignia on their berets, and a swastika on their arms.

We were handed over into their horrible hands. Screaming and waving their clubs, they counted 1,100 people, and they drove us into one wooden hut. That was our new residence.

The hut was flanked on two sides by rows of 3 stools, with a low setup called "heitzung"[15]. There was complete dead silence in the hut. A woman came in, mounted the low structure, and said in Hungarian: "Girls, you are all Hungarian, aren't you? For three years you lived a happy life. You had no interest in the fate of Slovakian girls. Now your time has arrived. You are now also here in good hands." Her eyes were glowing with revenge as she glared at us mercilessly.

She was an 18-year-old girl named "Leitner Miri"[16] and she was the commander of Bunk No.18 in Lager C.

---

[15] Heating in German – but of course there was no heating provided except the body heat of the person next to you.

[16] Miriam Leitner is also mentioned in Ruth Cohen's testimony documented in the US holocaust Museum. Life Changes — United States Holocaust Memorial Museum (ushmm.org)

When will I see my children?

What about my mother and sister?

We listened to her obscene words holding our tears back. Not a word was uttered by any of the 1,100 girls. Only one mother asked in the terrible silence: "What about my children? When will they be returned to me?" Another voice cried out, "When will I see my mother and sister?" Then we got the cruel answer: "Look outside" she said. We looked out the window and saw a huge flame coming out of the crematorium. She pointed in that direction. "Do you see that heavy smoke? That is your mother. The second is your father and in the third your children and your brothers are being burnt." At the time we thought that she was merely torturing us sadistically, but later we knew that was indeed the terrible truth. Millions of Jews were burnt in Europe, among them my beloved family and my precious children whom I had always protected.

While I am writing these lines, the pen is shaking in my hands and my eyes fill with tears. I keep wondering why I hadn't gone with them. Why was fate so cruel to me? These sights will be with me for the rest of my life. I was born only to suffer in this cruel world. I shall forever remember my beloved parents, my dear children who were torn out of my hands, clinging on to me desperately to the last minute. I am living in unbearable pain. I shall never be able to survive this, so why am I still living?

My mother suffered from terrible "survival guilt" which only subsided after she had 2 more sons after the end of War World II.

I will continue - the block commander tried to establish some order. "Go to sleep!" she yelled. "12 girls in one bed".

How? There were no beds. In the end we were beaten towards the rough unfinished wooden stools. We were pressed against each other like sardines. The night passed.

A loud bell clamored out at three in the morning. Some girls who had arrived there before us called out "dark shadow". I could not imagine what it was. Later, the SS taught us what it was. Within a few moments, everyone was driven out into the open yard at three in the morning. We were lined up five abreast and were carefully counted to make sure no one was missing. A loud command – "Achtung"[17] – was followed by complete silence. The 3,300 young girls were lined up in the yard. We were afraid to move when we heard the SS commander arriving.

---

[17] Attention! in German

The cruel and brutal SS woman "Graiza"

We were more afraid of the female commander than the male one. At her command, in the terrible rain, 3,300 people fell to their knees. This SS woman was called the beautiful "Graiza".[18] She was downright cruel, brutal, and capable of torturing people to death. We stood there for three hours without moving, twice a day. If someone was missing, the whole mass of people had to remain down on their knees for the whole day.

We then entered the bunk starving. We got neither bread nor water. We mounted the benches and then the midday meal was handed out – half a liter of watery soup with small pieces of potato or something hard floating around. 12 girls ate out of one pot – no spoon, no plate, and after five minutes the pot had to be returned empty.

At night we got one slice of bread with some margarine, and at 3 in the morning they gave us black bitter water, called coffee. This was our daily food ration which was not sustainable for anyone.[19] There was nothing to keep us

---

18

 Graiza – "Irma Grese" was a notorious concentration camp guard and warden who developed a reputation for taking a sadistic pleasure in her work. After the war, she was convicted of war crimes and executed by hanging.

https://en.wikipedia.org/wiki/Irma_Grese#Concentration_cam p_guard\

19 See References – Nutrition in Auschwitz-Birkenau

clean: no water, no soap, no towels. Peoples' health was ruined and destroyed, day by day.

A terrible disease spread among us. The lack of vitamins caused huge sores all over our bodies. The girls' teeth and hair fell out. There was no medication, no sanitary facilities - everything was filthy, and infections ran rampant among us.

We were in terrible fear of Dr. Mengele[20], who visited the camp every day. After each visit there were hundreds of victims, and nobody's life was safe. Every girl whom he touched could say goodbye to her comrades. In the daytime he selected his victims, and in the evening the black van [21] arrived and took them straight to the crematorium, which was burning day and night in frightful flames, turning hundreds of thousands of children into orphans.

The wind spread the smoke and the odor, and we knew sorrowfully that those were the burning bodies of our

---

[20] Josef Rudolf Mengele-also known as the Angel of Death-was a German *Schutzstaffel* (SS) officer and physician during World War II. He performed deadly experiments on twins and selected victims to be killed in the gas chambers,[a]
He was also one of the doctors who administered the poisonous gas. After World War II he hid in South America where the Israeli Mossad was trying to arrest him and bring him to justice. He suffered a stroke while swimming in a lake and died in 1979. His remains were positively identified in 1985. https://en.wikipedia.org/wiki/Josef_Mengele

[21] German records later showed that the Nazis used these black vans to poison their victims with exhaust gas coming from the car engine.

beloved ones and our brethren. Those were days of unbearable grief.

Six Months in Auschwitz with No End in Sight

I spent six long months in Auschwitz together with my younger sister, Miriam, and my sisters-in-laws, Esther, and Rivka.

October 31st, 1944 - We had been in the camp for 6 months and there was no prospect of our ever getting out of this cruel reality. We got up every morning at three o'clock and having no water to wash ourselves, no soap, and no towels, we wet our fingers with saliva and tried to wipe our eyes. We straightened the lice-infested garment in which we had slept and the four of us[22] went out hand in hand, not thinking that this day would be different from any previous one.

Midday - we were still in the same place, famished, having stood there since three in the morning. Then people dressed in civilian clothes arrived, accompanied by cruel Graiza, who started selecting the young ones for labor.

There was an outburst of anxiety, weeping and praying to God. I begged God not to separate me from my sister and sisters-in-law. We were indeed saved from separation, but many of our suffering compatriots were separated from their sisters. The camp was filled with wailing and howling. Thus, in a long line, our group started marching towards the railway station.

---

[22] The 4 women were: Bracha, her sister Miriam, and her two sisters-in-law Esther and Rivka

The freight train was already waiting for its victims. 150 people were packed into one compartment, without food or water. The horrors of the journey cannot be described. Some bread with a little butter was brought onto the train, but no water. We suffered terribly from thirst. The journey continued for two days and two nights. Only once was the door of the wagon opened – to remove the dead.

We arrived in Bergen Belsen[23]. We were very happy to have left the crematorium and the barbed wire. We were in the heart of a large forest. Day and night, we heard nothing but shooting. We were put in a cell, within a tent, where we were made to sit packed close to each other on the floor to make room for as many as possible. We sat there suffering day and night until God had mercy upon us and sent a strong storm which tore the tent into shreds. We remained under the bare sky in torrential rain. We were all freezing.

After that horrible night, when morning finally arrived, we were taken to a place with a roof where the situation was much better. We were only two in a bunk and were given a blanket to cover ourselves. The food here was as terrible as before. I was registered for work but my sister, Miriam, was very weak and I did everything I could to help her.

My job was to clean latrines, but I did it willingly. Those who worked got an extra slice of bread as well as another half a liter of soup. This addition saved my sister and my sisters-in-laws from starving. We remained there until December 17th ,1944.

Again, another selection was performed. We stood there all day in our light clothes, without moving, without food and without water. 800 people were required for labor, and we too were among that group. With God's mercy, we

---

[23] See Map 2 – Slave work Routes.

were not separated from each other. We marched through deep snow to the railway station. Again, as in the previous cases – a cattle car – no straw on the floor, no food, no water. Windows and doors were locked. There was no air and we arrived fainting.

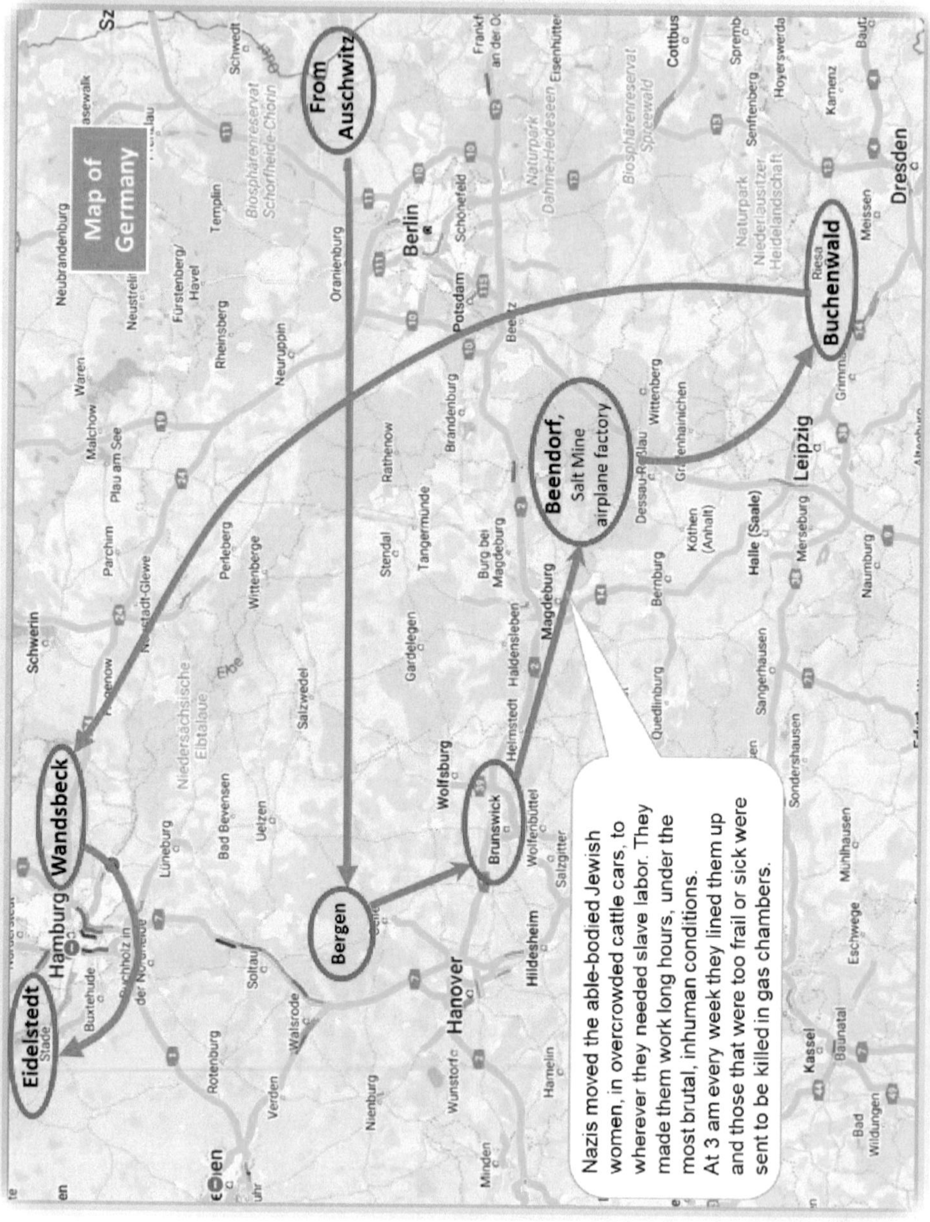
Map of Germany
From Auschwitz
Eidelstedt
Wandsbeck
Hamburg
Bergen
Brunswick
Beendorf,
Salt Mine
airplane factory
Buchenwald
Berlin
Leipzig
Dresden
Hanover
Magdeburg
Nazis moved the able-bodied Jewish women, in overcrowded cattle cars, to wherever they needed slave labor. They made them work long hours, under the most brutal, inhuman conditions.
At 3 am every week they lined them up and those that were too frail or sick were sent to be killed in gas chambers.

Map2 - Slave work Route

Frozen and Sick - Clearing Frozen Rubble in the middle of the Winter.

Braunschweig (Brunswick) – *a beautiful German city, demolished by the bombing. There was not one house that was undamaged. That was the reason 800 women were brought to clean up the debris. We now knew that this was the last road – we could not take any more. We were put into a huge stable - 800 women. Only half the stable was used since the other half had been ruined by the bombs. We lay down on the straw spread out on the floor that was already used by horses, and the concrete floor underneath was terribly cold. We spent 10 hard, bitter weeks there without any heat. They gave us one blanket to cover up five of us.*

We were woken up at 3:00 in the morning. Some black-colored water they called coffee was handed out. We drank it while standing in line and were marched off, with shovels on our shoulders and our feet wrapped in rags. We had no shoes. Our clothes were in shreds because we had not taken them off for ten weeks, night or day. The labor location was very far away, and it took an hour and a half to walk there. We were already exhausted when we arrived but were forced to start working immediately – to scoop out frozen bricks with a shovel and clear the debris. This went on day in and day out for ten weeks, no Sundays, no holidays. The citizens around pitied us and now and then threw down a piece of bread from a window. We got so hungry that we rummaged in the garbage bins and were delighted if we found a few potato peels or some rotting vegetables.

When we returned in the evening we were lined up in the deep snow and searched. If anyone was hiding a piece of potato or some roots, the SS women grabbed her head and beat it against the wall. They made her stand in the cold all night and the next day she did not get any food. The gnawing hunger was hardest to endure.

The evening meal was handed out as we entered the barn door, and we immediately mounted our bunks because there was no room to stand. Our hands were frozen. Sometimes we were unable to hold the plate and dropped it, thus remaining without the meager soup. Sleep was impossible because the bugs were swarming in the straw. We pulled out a hand full of lice from our body. Many, many were sick. Typhoid[24] spread and 10-20 people died every day. The feet of one miserable girl froze and she lay there on the bug-infested mattress until an infection set in and she died in terrible pain.

Both my sister, Miriam, and I got sick with typhoid. Our fever ran up to 40 degrees Celsius (104 Fahrenheit), *but we were strong and miraculously we survived.*

Obviously, they had no thermometers to measure temperatures, but this was an expression used by my mother to indicate that they had very high fevers.

We left that treacherous place after ten weeks, as spring was approaching. The Germans, fearing the infection spreading among the citizens, left the healthy workers in place, and the sick were taken to an extermination camp with the black van. Out of 800 women only 200 remained in ten weeks, most of them weak and with infected sores.

---

[24] **Typhoid fever** is a life-threatening infection caused by the bacterium SalmonellaTyphi. It is usually spread through contaminated food or water. Once bacteria are eaten or drunk, they multiply and spread rapidly into the bloodstream.

As the liberation was approaching, the Germans were frantic and began attending to our needs. We were given medication and bandages for the sores. Bombs were falling like rain and from time-to-time sirens were heard. But we were overjoyed. We felt our suffering was coming to an end. During the bombing, the SS women fled to the shelters, and we were free to pull out the lice from our clothes or search in the garbage cans for some potato peels to try and quiet our hunger.

Back in cattle cars

We were taken to work in a dangerous German underground salt mine factory.

The beginning of March - again we are in a cattle train, in deep distress, fearing that there will never be an end to our wandering. We were in terror of those cattle trains. After three days we arrived in Beendorf[25] where male and female SS were awaiting us. We were in terror of their cruelty.

We lived in a huge hall with barred windows and an iron door. It looked as though it was intended for robbers and murderers. But things looked much better. We were given clean clothes. We were delighted to get rid of the lice-infested clothes. We were given a regular bed, clean, with a good blanket. Oh God, to lie again in a clean bed after such a long time. We did not care about anything. We only wanted to be clean.

The commander was absolutely heartless. We were beaten regularly and every day a baton was broken on our backs. After two days of rest, we started working.

My dear younger sister, Miriam, was very weak. She could not bear the hunger, as we did. The work site was not far from our camp. When we arrived and saw where they brought us, we wanted to commit suicide. Good God, after such terrible suffering, we were standing in a salt quarry, 900 meters below the ground. We had to

---

[25] See Map2 – Slave work route.

walk for hours along serpentines full of pitfalls and steep stairs – up and down.

We arrived in a state very close to madness with the lice eating us up. We walked that path in the morning and evening. The hall that we worked in was well organized. The women were preparing parts of airplanes, and the men were mining salt. We spent two frightful months there. The men had lost any semblance of human beings. They looked like tortured skeletons.

At this point, the German war machine had started setting up factories in abandoned salt mines to avoid Allied bombing. They mercilessly utilized slave labor to continuously excavate more space for their factory expansion.[26]

We never saw daylight. The salt penetrated our sore feet, and the agony was unbearable. We lost all human resistance. Our lungs filled up with salt, our feet were swollen. We were no longer able to work, but they were driving us on with cruelty until we collapsed. Those who collapsed were put on stretchers and we had to carry these sick people up on those horrible steep serpentine steps.

---

[26] See References – Nazi Underground Factories

Gave the Kapo a hidden gold ring to save my sister's life.

My sister Miriam collapsed, and we were forced to carry her on a stretcher all that terrible way. I was watching my sister's pallid face all the time and was filled with horror that she may not be able to take this too much longer. It was there that she contracted tuberculosis.

I awoke one morning to a new reality… my only sister had lost consciousness. Heartbroken, I was chased out to go to work and leave my beloved sister to her fate. Trembling all day, I waited for evening to see her, but when I returned, she was gone.

She had been taken to hospital in Revirre, from where the sick were transferred in the black truck every day. I ran desperately from one place to the other, trying to find out some information. I had two wedding bands which I had managed to hide, knowing that when in danger of death they might save us, and we might be able to escape.

Having read this narrative, I frequently contemplate how my mother succeeded in concealing valuable gold rings after being forcibly stripped naked and provided with only rags to wear. I can only surmise that she must have ingested the rings and later recovered them. I greatly admire her capacity for forethought, her resilience, and her unwavering determination to survive and safeguard her beloved sister.

I handed over those rings to a woman and she managed to save my sister from death. Miriam remained with me, deadly pale, with a fever of 40 degrees Celsius (104-degree Fahrenheit), *without medication, unable to swallow the soup. She was given a small summer garment to leave the hospital in Revere and everything else she had was taken from her.*

In the morning, we had to go back again to work underground. We prayed to God to take us both together. We could not bear this any longer. Suddenly, we were ordered to leave even that cursed place. Where to? Even the Germans did not know. The whole country was already besieged by their enemies. We were dizzy from the heavy bombing and could hear the noise of the hateful train in which we suffered so many agonizing and terrifying days and weeks. Its many dangers still loomed ahead of us. Again, 200 people were forced into a cattle wagon.

There we met German criminals who were in prison for murder. They decided to torture us to death to make more room for themselves. For many long days we travelled in hunger and thirst. The young girls were so thirsty that they drank their own urine. They were going mad. Those cursed Germans pressed us together so strongly that we had to stand on each other's feet. Those who collapsed with weakness were immediately trampled to death.

The men were also brought into the wagon. Our thirst and hunger were unbearable. People were collapsing. With a little water they might have survived, but the criminals did not care. Jews were left to perish. Every night some eight or ten people were beaten to death. In the morning the tortured dead bodies with shattered skulls were thrown out. We were forced to see those sights and be terrified to death, thinking that our turn would come the following night.

There was an insane look on every face. Our hair was standing on end, our mouths were full of sores, our eyes were bulging out of their sockets and our swollen feet could not carry us. This hell lasted 14 days and nights. After a few days we were ordered to get off. We were told that we would get food. There was a glimmer of hope in our eyes extinguished with tears, hope for a piece of bread and a drop of water. "Oh God", we cried, we will get bread and water. I embraced my sister and begged her to hold out only a short time, until we were saved.

But the truth was different. We were terribly disappointed. There was no food. Instead of bread we were given uncooked potatoes, and many did not even get that. We were no longer praying for life but for death. We begged God to put an end to our suffering. "Dear God, let us die at your hand and not at the hands of these merciless murderers."

A beastly scream was heard issuing orders. That day a rumor was whispered around that the Germans had got an order to kill us all since there was no more food. We were too weak to cry or to encourage each other as we had been trying to do in the past. There was no need for encouragement, we were prepared for anything. We waited for the last second, and indeed it arrived.

<u>This is the end – no more food left – everyone will be shot.</u>

Everyone got off the train and stood in groups of 100. As space was scarce, we were made to sit down on the dead and trample them. They were thrown off the train like stones. This was a horrific sight, but we did not feel any pain anymore. We waited for the end. A few hours passed until 6000 people stood up in groups of 100. We were in an open field under the bare sky. It was frightful to see the machine guns aiming directly at us.

And then the miracle occurred, a miracle sent by God. A soldier came running at the last moment and called out breathlessly: "Everyone back. Food has arrived!" We did not have any emotions left; to be happy or sad that we were saved. We returned to the wagons. There was more room because the sick and the dead had been thrown off.

After 5 days on the train, we were given some bread which we could hardly swallow, our mouths dry and full of sores. Night had fallen when the train started moving. We arrived in the morning, exhausted, full of lice, to Buchenwald[27] – the fearsome and treacherous camp. This was a gigantic camp of men, whose appearance cannot be described – men who had lost any human semblance. They had gone through the most terrible abuse and were forced to work beyond their strength. Hundreds died every day. The lice[28] brought painful sores and the sores got infected and

---

[27] See Map2 - Slave work Route.

[28] Lice - are tiny insects (about 3mm in length) that feed on human blood several times a day. They live inside clothing and hair strands and their tiny bite into the skin produces itching and allergic reaction. Scratching the itching skin can produce infections.

infections caused numerous deaths. Throughout the two weeks on the train, people did not wash. A blood infection spread, and people kept dying like flies.

In the woods, under pouring rain and wet to the bones, we stood from morning till nightfall, shivering in the cold. A bowl of warm soup was finally handed out. We took shelter under the cattle train wagon to eat our soup there. My dear sister, whom I had been carrying on my back for three days and three nights, was so weak that she could barely eat the warm soup. The soup revived her a little and she whispered in a barely audible voice "God bless you for this, it was very tasty." It was not possible to return to the wagon because the roof was open, and it was full of water.

Under the train I made some room for my sick sister. I did not sleep at all that night, trying all the time to make sure that she was still breathing. We thought we would all perish there. But on the sixth day the sky cleared and immediately air raid and air sirens were heard. The Germans were anxious to take the train outside the Buchenwald camp, but there was nowhere for them to escape. The whole camp was already surrounded by their enemies.

Again, we stood in the open fields under the bare sky for 2 days. Suddenly the SS soldiers were informed that there was another small camp which could hold the captives for some time. Again, we marched in the pouring rain, a blanket over our heads, and reached Wansbeck[29], where we were met with terrible cruelty.

---

[29] Wansbeck Is near Hamburg, Germany.

German criminals released from prison are now with us and they terrorize us.

Again, we were with the German criminals released from prison and they, of course, were first in everything. We stood outside, shivering, and tired. One girl fainted and fell. The block commander fell upon her like a cruel animal. Caught her by the neck and started shaking her and kicking her pitilessly; then took off in anger. This went on until nightfall.

They were taking revenge on everyone because they felt they were trapped[30]. We spent 10 days in this camp. On the second day after our arrival, 6 German criminal prisoners fled. The commander said that if they were not caught by nightfall, 10 women from every nationality would be shot. As the escaped prisoners were German, they finally gave up on this penalty.

Our hunger was so strong that we used every opportunity to find some food. We went out into the court and there we could smell sardines. We dug into the ground with our nails and indeed we found a hidden treasure of tiny sardines full of clay. I do not know how it got there. Probably the area had a food pantry that got bombed. The Germans caught us and did not allow us to eat the meager dirty sardines, claiming that it was poisoned food. They claimed that if we ate the food, we would infect them.

We were beaten mercilessly, and they would not allow us to go out in the courtyard again. The German guards were

---

[30] At this point the Allied armies were surrounding the area and the Germans felt trapped and out of control.

getting scared from the approaching Allied armies. *They ate our rations as well, and with the rest of our food they bought clothes* (prisoners' clothing) *in which they were planning to escape.*

Ten days passed in misery and one day we were told that all the Jews should line up in groups of 50. We asked where we were being taken and the answer was: to Himmel camp[31]. Any piece of clothing that had some value was taken from us as, in the Himmel camp, there would not be any need for clothing. Two SS soldiers with bayonets were assigned to each group of 50. We were terribly frightened. The four of us held hands all the time. We were afraid that the merciless murderers were going to kill us all.

---

[31] This was a camp inside the city of Hamburg, Germany -see Map2.

<u>Chapter 3 – Liberation</u>

We are riding in a passenger train not in cattle cars.

Within the great fear, a miracle occurred. We were commanded to get on the train, but we could not believe our eyes. We saw a passenger train instead of the cattle cars. We were afraid to get into the beautiful second-class compartment of a beautiful passenger train. We had not seen such a train in a whole year. This trip was the last one in our journey of torment after our many days of agony. During this time, we were hungry, thirsty, infested with lice and broken in spirit. In this condition they had made us cross the whole of Germany.[32]

Finally, we got on this passenger train, and we looked at each other. Is it possible that filthy, and dressed in rags, we were traveling in such a beautiful train?

The destination was reached after an hour, and we awoke from the beautiful dream to a horrible reality. Again, the loud command "Everybody Down!!!". The group started marching. After an hour we came to a place called Eidelstedt,[33] (Hamburg, Germany) *a small place where the other Jewish prisoners had been gathered. We remained there famished for two days. Two people got a ladle of soup to split between them. I sneaked to the garbage pile to take out anything I could find – some*

---

[32] See Map2 showing the Journey of Torments.
[33] Eidelstedt is a quarter of Hamburg, Germany. It is located on the northwestern boundaries of the borough and of the city.

cabbage leaves, some potato peels, and tree leaves, anything I could give my perishing sister.

One morning I awoke to great excitement. It was whispered that we were being handed over to the Red Cross and we would be liberated. All our optimism had died already. We could no longer believe that after the horrors of the past year, we too would be free. We could not believe that after the terrors and dangers, we would finally be able to leave that treacherous, murderous, concentration camp.

The great day had arrived. Again, we had to march, but this time we were marching with a light heart, under the command of the last guards.

The guards that escorted us were no longer the SS, but regular German soldiers wearing a white band around their sleeves. Again, we were commanded to get on freight trains. O God, how terrible. Where, where does this road lead us? This time there were only 50 people in a wagon and the floor was covered with straw. We were also given some bread for the journey and a bit of canned meat. We saw that our situation was improving. We realized with satisfaction that our escorts were treating us decently. They were eager to convince us that the passage through Denmark will lead to freedom. This made our hearts beat with a little hope, but we still feared that we were just being transferred to another concentration camp.

The doors of the wagons were not closed. Pure air was blowing in and through the opening we could see the beautiful countryside views. We no longer saw bombed out buildings. There were no sights of terrible destruction. We saw beautiful blossoming spring flowers and green pastures.

Yet our hearts were still beating with fear. It was hard to imagine and believe that after so much suffering, the flowers could also bloom for us on this beautiful spring day.

I continue to marvel, and I am amazed at the incredible optimism and remarkable spirit that enabled my mother to set aside her nightmares and appreciate the beauty of the blossoming spring flowers.

This ability to admire and enjoy the beauty of the moment, while being taken in a miserable cattle car to an unknown destination, exemplified the strength that allowed her to survive and recover from the horrors of the Holocaust.

Arrived in Denmark –

We could not believe that people were welcoming us with food.

Meanwhile the train arrived in the small Danish border town of Padborg[34] and stopped at the small train station.

The whole town, including children and old people, were there at the railway station to welcome us with gift packages. Dear God, is this true? We were not being handed over to the SS, but to good, kindhearted people. Red Cross nurses were embracing us compassionately while we were covered with rags held together with pins…no, this cannot be… this is only a dream… this is much more than what the sick and broken heart is able to grasp.

We embraced each other again and again and could not stop crying with joy. There was a gleam of joy even in my dear sick sister Miriam's eyes. When she got off the train, the poor soul was so weak that she fell. If I had not seen that, the crowd would have trampled her in a minute. Rivka, my young sister-in-law, had a crying fit from all the excitement around her and she looked very sick. One of the Red Cross nurses jumped onto the train, held her, and tried to comfort her. But Rivka's weeping became louder and louder, and we all started weeping uncontrollably with joy.

---

[34] Padborg is a southern Danish border town located on the border with Germany. See Map 3 – Liberation.

Large white vans, with a huge red cross, like in the stories, came to pick up the sick. Inside the wagon we were smothered with masses of white bread, cakes, chocolate… like the manna from the heaven. White handkerchiefs were waving to welcome us. We were feeling sick with exhilaration.

The Red Cross vans were all over to give us first aid. Nurses dressed in white and Danish men bearing a Red Cross band on their sleeves put their arms around the sick and gently helped them get into the vans. Stretchers arrived and the small ambulance was going back and forth. I wanted to jump off the train and thank every one of them separately, to shout out: "Kind souls, we are forever grateful to you. You have saved our lives… Can you imagine what it means to be released from a concentration camp and escape from the SS?" No! I thought to myself, anyone who had not been through those experiences could never imagine or understand these horrors.

I was deep in my thoughts when I heard a soft voice calling us: children, we are going to the restaurant for lunch. Dear God, the Danish people will probably never forget what they saw when we arrived. The lice were crawling all over our clothes. We were wearing huge wooden shoes and were covering ourselves in rough blankets instead of coats. And yet they embraced us with gentle, loving hands and took us by the hand to the lunchroom. When we arrived, they surrounded us with unimaginable love. With tearful eyes and broken hearts, we realized that after years of abysmal hatred, and unimaginable suffering, we could still have feelings, when surrounded by immense love that radiates so much compassion.

We are Human Beings again,

with Names not Slaves with Tattooed Numbers.

We were emerging from a constant feeling of numbness. Our minds had been drugged. Throughout the year we had been given bromine[35]. Our minds were not functioning. Only now were we beginning to shake off the influence of the drug.[36] The pain of our bereavement was dawning on us. **We are human beings again! We are FREE.**

Where are my beloved parents who had bestowed endless love upon us, like these people who are total strangers? As I look back, I see the crowd and I search for my dear little sons –Tibike and my sweet Pityuka. I felt them being torn away from me - then I woke up. No - this was exactly a year ago - that awful day. Now I am not able to bear this terrible pain. The pain is much stronger now. We are now standing orphaned, torn away from all our beloved ones.

We were being taken broken-hearted, desolate, and tortured but full of hope - to a beautiful restaurant with nicely set tables. Merciful young girls and mature women from the Red Cross were serving us. They gave us bread

---

[35] It is not clear if it was bromine or some other substance that the Nazis put in their food for medical experimentation. Many of the women prisoners stopped having menstrual cycles and, after liberation many were unable to have any children.

[36] Bromine solution of potassium, sodium and calcium was commonly used during that period as a sedative, very much like barbiturates.

as white as snow, butter, wonderful coffee which never ran out. I clapped my hands. Oh God, we are given real coffee!!

I ran happily to my ailing sister and offered her a cup, but poor thing, she was unable to drink even coffee. My God! After such a year, to sit at a table and have a real supper!

After the meal we were taken gently and lovingly to the place where we would spend the night, but we were too excited, and we could not fall asleep. Within a single day, our lives had changed so drastically. All night long we were murmuring prayers of thanks to our Creator for the great miracle he had bestowed on us. In the morning, after a long sleepless night, we were again called to a rich, tasty breakfast. We could not yet believe that everything around us was real. We were afraid that this beautiful dream would turn into another cruel reality. With God's mercy, our beautiful dream was a reality.

Even today it is hard for me to grasp how this miracle happened. We could not - we really could not believe it. We stayed one more day in this enchanting, unforgettable place in Denmark. We were embraced with immense love, and after being surrounded with gentleness and given all kinds of sweet goodies, we were again seated in the Red Cross cars and taken to the railway station. We were told that we were going to Sweden where we would also be in the care of the Red Cross.

There were still SS soldiers walking around, but we looked at them with open scorn, our heads held high. We felt that under the protection of the Red Cross, they were no longer a threat to us. Again, we mounted a second-class cabin in a beautiful train. The compartments were full of gift packages.

These European trains were arranged in private compartments that seated 4-6 people. There was a corridor with windows on one side connecting all those compartments. These compartments could also turn into bunk beds, each accommodating four sleeping people.

When the train started moving, while waving our hands, we felt that we were forever indebted to these noble Danish souls. Red Cross nurses in white uniforms were tending to us, since we were all sick. Every ten minutes someone entered the compartment to ask whether we needed anything or whether we were perhaps hungry. My God! For the first time in years, we could refuse food. No, We Were Not Hungry.

For the journey, we received so many packages filled with delicious foods that our shrunken stomach could not accept. We all became sick from eating so much food.

On a ship headed for freedom

The first time we boarded the ship, a sharp pain pierced my heart. I went up on the deck, isolated from everyone, and awoke in the pure air.

These are large ferry boats that run across the bay, between different islands of Denmark and Sweden.

We were on board a luxury boat with waiters in tuxedoes serving us while we were still huddled in coarse blankets, void of any human shape. With lice still crawling all over us, we were still living the horrors of the concentration camp.

I stood on the deck looking at the majestic sea with its splendid waves reflecting in the light. My heart was torn with the thought that I had always dreamt of sailing with my dear husband in such a boat.

My mother's dream of sailing with her husband on a beautiful ship finally came true many years later when she emigrated to the US and crossed the Atlantic Ocean on a small cruise ship.

I was staring at the blue sky and saw the beautiful seashore approaching. Those moments were full of longing for my husband. Oh my God, we were so painfully torn apart. We had been ripped apart for two years and there was not much hope that we would ever see each other again.

When the boat sailed into the port of Copenhagen, people were waiting for us with gift packages. The kind Red Cross workers were also there to help us. We spent several hours in this beautiful capital. Many photographers took pictures of us in our miserable attire, every second from a different angle.

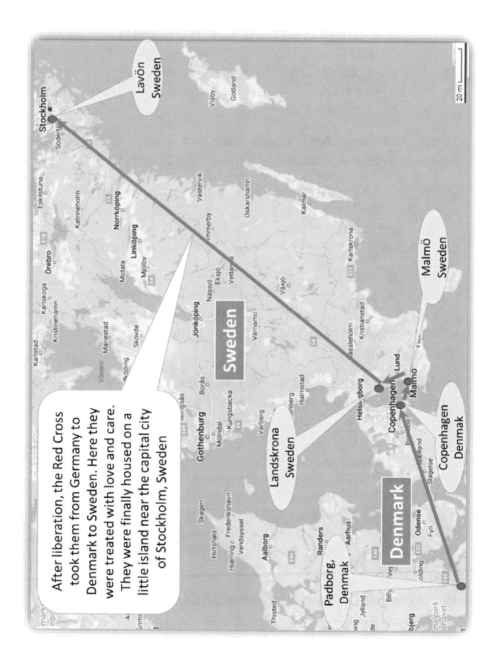

Map 3 - Liberation

The Swedish Red Cross representatives greeted us, and we came under their protection and care. We boarded a Swedish boat and enjoyed the thoughts that in this peaceful, calm country, we will never meet those SS soldiers who brought upon us this horrible tragedy.

End of the War –

Germany Surrendered – Hitler is Dead.

From out at sea, we saw the electric lights reflected from Sweden. Suddenly there was a great uproar, and everybody was shouting with joy: "Germany has surrendered!" "Germany has surrendered!"

37

On April 30, 1945, Hitler committed suicide. Within days, Berlin fell to the Soviet army.

---

37 Wikipedia – Victory in Europe Day

On May 8, 1945, World War II in Europe ended. As the news of Germany's surrender reached the rest of the world, joyous crowds gathered to celebrate in the streets, clutching newspapers that declared Victory in Europe (V-E Day).

Overjoyed, we entered the port city of Malmö[38] and from there we were taken to the city of Lund.
We were taken to a gorgeous palace made of glass to take a bath. We got soft towels, all sorts of bath soaps, beautiful clothes, underwear, and shoes.
We were dressed from head to toe. The clothes were too large. We were all skin and bones. I weighed 41kilos (90lb)*, my younger sister, Miriam, weighed 39 kilos* (86lb)*, my sister-in-law, Esther, weighed 33 kilos* (73lb) *and Rivka weighed 38 kilos* (84lb).

We felt we were born anew because the clean clothes were like balm to our bodies, tormented with sores. We drove to a close-by small town called Landskrona[39].

---

[38] The Swedish city of Malmö is about 10 miles across the bay from Copenhagen.

[39] Landskrona is a town on the Swedish coast. It possesses an excellent natural port, which has lent the town first military and then commercial significance. Ferries operate from Lankdskrona to several islands and to the Danish capital of Copenhagen.

People were marching in the street all night with torches in their hands, celebrating the end of the war. This was a most exciting sight. Never in my life have I seen anything more beautiful.

Here we were put on a strict diet and for a while the sick were cared for. I was also treated, and we were quarantined for 3 weeks. I had a huge sore on my leg, deep down into the bone and an infection had set in. The other women were also covered with large sores, and we were all treated.

My sister Miriam is treated in a Swedish hospital.

As we were coming out of the quarantine, I experienced some very sad days. On the last quarantine day my dear sister was taken to a hospital. I cried bitterly when I parted from her. Dear God, I thought in fright, in the camps we had always been together, hand in hand, so that they would not separate us.

Now, when the time that we had longed for so much finally arrived, we were forced to part. I fainted when the Red Cross car left with my beloved, terribly ill sister. The kind, good-hearted nurses took care of me and tried to comfort me.

She was no longer in the hands of Germans, they said, these kind people would surely try to cure her. They calmed me and cried together with me.

I told them of the terrible tragedy of my life. Of all my beautiful and large family, only my sister survived, and she too was sick with tuberculosis. The doctors had already given up on her. Many days passed in deep despair. The kind Red Cross nurses were bringing news often[40] about my sister.

---

[40] Miriam was in an isolated tuberculosis clinic which allowed no visitors. The only way of communication was by somebody coming over with a verbal or written message.

Bracha became a nurse-aid in order to help her sister and others who still needed to recover from their horrible tragedies.

She looks confident and ready to help the sick people in the hospital.

The noble Swedish folk made great efforts to help us forget the horrors we had gone through. They did wonders for us since in a few weeks we gained 10 kilos (22 lb). *My dear sister's health was also improving and there was hope that she would recover. People left the quarantine healthy.*

Miriam recovered from tuberculosis and was able to return and stay with her sister in the camp near the capital city of Stockholm.

My two young sisters-in-law and I were staying in a camp close to Stockholm. Every day we went to the unbelievably beautiful Swedish capital[41]. It meant a lot to us that everyone was surrounding us with love. Here no one hated us. It was a place full of peace, quiet and tranquility. The war remained only in our bleeding hearts, where peace will never return.

From left to right

Esther, Bracha and Rivka

They are in Sweden standing in front of their Barrack #13 all dressed up for a picture.

Heartbroken, we walked around in the streets of the capital. People were living with their families while we, with tears in our eyes, felt that we did not belong to anyone. We are like wandering dogs, without a home, without a

---

[41] Seeing the beautifully illuminated capital city of Stockholm must have been magical since they came from a little Romanian village which at that time did not even have electricity.

*homeland. Pressing our hands to our forehead **we remembered that each of us is merely a number.***

*My left arm bears the number **A10257** and the memory of the German concentration camp will remain forever on my arm with their tattoo. Our real tragedy was only beginning.*

Esther had **A10264** and Rivka had **A10265** tattooed on her left arm.

We are now living in Lovön[42], in the woods. Everything is so beautiful around here. Ten girls are sharing a room. We are attached to each other like real sisters, all sharing a sad life story. I was the only one married. The others were all young, single girls.

---

[42] Lovön is on an island very close to Stockholm.

Dear God – Did anybody in my family survive?

The days pass in anxiety. Oh God, will we ever hear that postal connections with Romania have started? Are we ever going to hear news from our loved ones? Then one beautiful day the postal service with Romania started to work. Information was beginning to arrive.

There was great joy in the camp. Before going to bed, each of us prayed to God every night. "Dear God, please bring us a telegram in the morning."

Sending a telegram in those days was a costly and labor-intensive process. One had to go to the main post office and write a brief message on paper. The paper was then given to a telegraph operator who transmitted the message letter by letter to the telegraph office closest to the destination address. Once it arrived at the destination telegraph office, it was printed, put in an envelope, and sent by mail to the destination address. This process took a few days, but it was the fastest means of sending a message at the time.

Every day passed with anxiety and fear. Many girls were receiving telegrams and we rejoiced, or felt their pain, and cried with them. Each telegram was a spark of hope for a new life and a new beginning for us. Perhaps we can also have a future. Perhaps tomorrow? Each of us wondered whether the next telegram would arrive for us.

The days passed and I became very depressed. The girls who were with me tried to comfort me. I did not want to go on living because there was no purpose to my life. There was nothing and nobody to live for. My dear sister was still in hospital, and I heard nothing from my beloved family.

<u>Finally - a telegram from my beloved husband</u>

On June 12th, 1945, I woke up with a heavy feeling. I was alone in the room; the girls had gone out to work. Early in the morning I felt that this day was going to be different from the other days. They rang the gong for lunch.

This is when the mail is handed out. We are all eager, running, trembling with excitement. I too was eager like the others. Suddenly I heard a voice calling: Borbala [43] Goldstein, a telegram for you. I fainted. The girl standing next to me caught me, took the telegram and read aloud the following incredible words:
"I am feeling all right! I am waiting for you! Come immediately! Herman Goldstein!"

I mustered all my strength and full of joy, I tore the telegram from her hands and held it close. I looked at the signature, for I could not believe my ears. Yes, I see it with my own eyes: **Herman Goldstein.**
Yes, it was Herman (Tzvi), *my dear beloved husband. I thank you dear God, that he is alive, and he is calling me to come back home. My dear kind husband. My heart started pounding and the voice of life was whispering: "Yes, you must live. Your spouse is calling for you."*

I often wondered how my father managed to find the address for the telegram he sent to his beloved wife. In the post-war period, survivors were scattered across various Displaced Persons Camps throughout Europe.

---

[43] Her Hungarian name was Boris. Her English Name was Barbara, and her Hebrew name was Bracha.

I believe that my mother may have sent a postcard to her former home address, hoping that someone who had survived would come across it and contact her in Sweden. Her husband, Tzvi, survived the war and returned to his old address in Romania. There he most probably found the postcard with his beloved wife's Swedish address.

From left to right, Esther, Bracha and Rifka in Sweden reading the telegram.

Like bad tidings, good tidings do not come alone. Good news followed good news. My brothers-in-laws, and my younger brother – dear Gyula, (Julius) *all came back. He spent two years of suffering in the Ukraine.*

I have one more prayer to God: give us back my youngest brother Jozsi[44], who was also taken to a slave labor camp.

Second on the bottom left is Bracha and her sister Miriam is next to her.

In Sweden at some celebration. One can clearly see the young people (refugees) sitting at the table and standing are the Swedish older people providing them the meals.

---

[44] Jozsi (or Josef) was Bracha's youngest brother, who was very close to her. He never returned from the Hungarian slave labor camp. We must assume that he died during the war. He was a very handsome young man as seen in one surviving photograph.

34-year-old Bracha on the right with her 30-year-old sister Miriam on the left.
This picture was taken in March 1946 in Sweden one year after her liberation.

Notice that Miriam is already proudly showcasing her Jewish identity by wearing a
Star of David necklace.

It is truly remarkable that after being terrorized by the Nazis for being Jewish,
Miriam has the courage and the moral strength to openly express her pride in her
Jewish identity.

*All the others – my dearly beloved parents, my sisters and
my two handsome boys, whom I had shielded as long as I
could - I have no hope for. They were murdered in front of
our eyes by the brutal German criminals and there was no
hope of ever seeing them alive again.*

*I wish to end this small story with a **blessing for the noble Swedish nation**. On behalf of refugees who are indebted to you forever –*

***May God bless you for all the kindness you bestowed on us.**[45]*

As for myself, the writer of these pages, I beseech those who may read these lines, not to pass judgment on me. This is the story of an unfortunate mother, whose heart will forever ache, longing for her two small, beautiful, beloved sons. A wife who is full of anxiety, going back home to her husband alone, without her children.

Boris Bauer (Bauer was her original maiden's name)

Boris Goldstein Wife of Herman Goldstein[46]

---

[45] In her original memoir, my mother rightfully blessed the Swedish nation because of the kindness and help they gave her, but why did she not curse the Nazi's for their crimes? See Chapter 5 for some explanations.

[46] Bracha signed her memoir in Hungarian as "Goldstein Hermanne" which translates as the wife of Herman Goldstein.
Her use of this married synonym was a way of saying that despite losing most of her family, she is not totally alone. She lost her children, but she has a loving husband waiting for her.

Chapter 4 -The Rest of Bracha's Story

Help from the King of Sweden

(story told by Dora Shoen)

In the aftermath of World War II, most of Europe lay in ruins, and chaos was widespread. Millions of survivors and refugees were attempting to return to whatever remained of their homes and hometowns, in desperate attempts to reunite with loved ones who might have also survived.

As soon as postal services were restored, people began sending postcards and telegrams to their old addresses, in the hope that relatives, friends, or acquaintances might find the mail and respond. That is how my father was able to discover that his wife Bracha, survived the war and was now in Sweden along with Miriam, Esther, and Rifka.

He immediately sent a telegram to that Swedish postal address, informing his wife that he, too, has miraculously survived, and was eagerly anticipating their reunion. My mother fainted when she received the telegram. Imagine her emotional state at that moment when she learned that her beloved husband survived following all the horrors that she witnessed.

After expending almost superhuman efforts surviving the German extermination machine along with her sister and sisters-in-law, my mother now concentrated her efforts on effecting a reunion with her husband. Initially, she felt that it would be best for him to join her in Sweden, where people are wonderful, and where they could start a new life in a wonderful country.

Further, she felt that returning to her native town in Romania would be nothing but a continuous, agonizing reminder of her tragedy, and of the brutal murder of her parents, siblings, and children.

My father responded that he had been able to return to their little home back in Romania. Although the house had been looted and ransacked by soldiers and neighbors, he had, nevertheless, found old photos, and recovered some of their furniture, dishes, and household goods. They could restart their new life in the same home where they lived before the war. Besides, he explained, he didn't speak Swedish, didn't know anything about the Swedish culture, and would find it impossible to establish a business there.

Whereas, in their old hometown, he explained, he found his father's old book/newspaper/tobacco store[47] that was relatively intact and salvageable. He was now planning to reopen the store, along with his older brothers Moses (Moric in Hungarian) and Max (Menyus in Hungarian), who had also survived the Holocaust.

Although my mother desperately wished to re-start her married life with her beloved husband, she remained, nevertheless, terrified of the memories and nightmares the old village sites might reawaken for her. She feared that returning to her village in Romania, with its empty streets

---

[47] Tzvi's father owned a small general store in town where he sold small household items, newspapers, books, and mostly tobacco products. In those days, since almost everyone smoked cigarettes, selling cigars and tobacco was a very lucrative business.

and homes, would be a constant, painful, reminder of the loving family members – parents, brothers, sisters, and sons – who were gone forever. These thoughts were incredibly frightening to her and fueled her reluctance to return to her native village.

As their wedding anniversary approached, my father tried to create a plan to bring his beloved wife back home. With my mother in Sweden and my father in the Romania how can they celebrate such an important event?

My father had always been a strong believer in celebrating special events such as birthdays and anniversaries. Now that the war was over and the Germans were defeated, he couldn't fathom not celebrating his wedding anniversary with his wife. But how could this be done?

He came up with a brilliant idea. He created a composite picture[48], from two individual photos taken in different places, and sent it to his wife for their wedding anniversary.

---

[48] This was equivalent to today's computer generated photoshop overlays. Computers had not yet been invented at that time, and this picture was done with manual cut and photo overlays techniques.

	To Borbala Goldstein; Võxjõ, Sweden[49];
Back of the picture In Hungarian	With all my love; Herman ; Valea lui Mihai; March 30, 1946

Here is the composite picture created by my father and sent to his wife in Sweden for their wedding aniversary.

---

[49] This could have been a central post office address set up for handling mail distribution to known refugees in Sweden.

My mother's picture was taken in Sweden and my father's picture was taken in Romania.

Note that the background in the picture depicts very distorted shadows of human faces. These symbolize and represent the human beings tortured during the holocaust.

With these shadows my father relayed a very powerful message to his wife:

"Let's put our tragedy behind us and let's start a new life together!"

My mother was so touched by this loving anniversary gift that she could no longer resist her husband's siren call. Despite the nightmares, she resolved to return to her husband, in her native Romanian village.

But how could that be done when she was living solely on Red Cross charity?

The Swedish Red Cross provided their daily food, shelter, and clothing. She had no money or means for travelling 2,700 km to the other end of the European continent. Her situation was made even more challenging by the high inflation and the exorbitant cost of living immediately after World War II.

While discussing her dilemma with the other women in her Swedish barracks, a wild idea was generated. "What about asking the King of Sweden for help"? suggested one of her friends.

"The Swedish people have been so very kind and so very generous, maybe their king will be just as nice?"

My mother was dubious, saying,

"Are you kidding? How can I, a nobody - a poor Jewish woman who survived Auschwitz, approach a king?"

"Well, since it will only cost you a stamp and an envelope, what do you have to lose?" said the friend. "Miracles can happen". "See how all of us in this barrack are living, walking, miracles. Everyone here is a witness to the miracle of her own personal survival."

My mother eventually agreed to try it, acknowledging, "Okay, I suppose it can't hurt to try, but I don't speak or write in Swedish, and my handwriting is not so great."

"Well, talk to Dora"[50] said the friend "she was a legal secretary back in Romania, and she is fluent in both German and Swedish. Maybe she can compose and write a letter in your name."

Dora turned out to be a wonderful compassionate person who was in the same camp with my mother, and she agreed to help any way she could. Dora collected her thoughts, and composed an impassioned letter, in my mother's name, addressed to his Majesty Gustaf V, King of Sweden.

---

[50] Dora Shoen was with my mother in the Nazi death camps and in Sweden. Dora was the person who typed up my mother's memoir, since she was a skilled legal secretary. She was fluent in multiple languages, and she knew how to type well.

See Chapter 10 on Dora Shoen and her video interview.

51

His Majesty
King Gustav V of
Sweden

In her letter, Bracha
asked the King to
help her get back to
her surviving
husband in Romania.

In the letter she recounted my mother's tragic experiences during the Holocaust, including the loss of her children, parents, and numerous family members. She revealed the remarkable news that Bracha's beloved husband had also survived the war and was currently waiting for her in their native Romanian village.

---

51 Wikipedia – Gustaf V - King of Sweden from 8 December 1907 until his death in 1950.
Gustaf V attempted to convince Hitler during a visit to Berlin to soften his persecution of the Jews, according to historian Jörgen Weibull. He was also noted for appealing to the leader of Hungary to save its Jews "in the name of humanity."

With a burning desire to reunite with her husband, my mother requested the king's assistance in finding employment that would enable her to save enough money to purchase a train ticket and return to her husband in Romania.

Dora typed this letter on an ancient mechanical typewriter in the Red Cross office. As a legal secretary, Dora was an excellent typist who spoke many languages and she had been working in that office.

Interestingly, this same Dora used that very same office typewriter to transcribe Bracha's memoir, which serves as the foundation for this book. If you look at Appendix A you can see a copy of the original typewritten memoir, in Hungarian, which Dora typed up on long legal papers. This original typed document is now preserved in the Yad Vashem historical archive.

My mother put the typed letter in an envelope, added her name with her return address on the left upper corner. The envelope had no street or city destination address, just the name King Gustaf V. She put a stamp on the upper right corner, sealed the envelope and mailed it, convinced that she would never receive a reply.

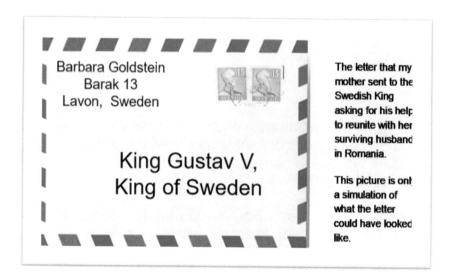

The Royal Gift

A few weeks later two men in uniforms showed up at her bunk door, inquiring about Barbara (Bracha) Goldstein. My mother, conditioned to be terrified of men in uniform, became paralyzed and froze in fear. She hesitated to reveal her identity. In the past, the sight of men in uniform had always signaled the arrival of devastating news for her.

Horrible thoughts flashed though her mind. "I might have addressed the King improperly". "Maybe it's even a crime to address the King in this country". "Who knows what Swedish laws I may have inadvertently violated. They may throw me in jail, or even worse, for this!"

52

Two young man from the Swedish Kings Royal Guards, in their normal military uniforms looking for my mother.

This is only a typical picture of the Royal Guards not the actual picture taken at the time of this event.

After the uniformed men asked for Barbara Goldstein for the third time, my mother finally mustered enough courage to admit that she was indeed the person they were looking for.

Observing her profound fear, one of the men approached and spoke gently, saying, "His majesty - Our King - received your letter and he is sending you a gift. Here are pre-paid train and ferry tickets, which will enable you to return to Romania and reunite with your beloved husband."

---

52 Wikipedia – Swedish Royal Guards

These are simulated set of tickets that could have been given by the King of Sweden to Bracha.

These tickets allowed her to return from Sweden to her beloved husband in Romania.

He handed the envelope to a thoroughly astonished Bracha who could not believe her eyes and ears. Overwhelmed emotionally, she started crying. Friends embraced her saying "we told you that miracles could happen."

Then, the second uniformed man stepped forward and with an equally gentle voice said, "Here is a gift from the King of Sweden, so you will not return empty-handed to your husband. It is a set of silverware, bearing the King's personal monogram. Please present it to your husband when your return home."

At that point, my mother's emotions overwhelmed her completely. She broke down and burst into uncontrolled tears. All her fellow refugees hugged her, surrounded her with love and encouraging words. "Is this truly real or am I just dreaming? "She asked.

The King of Sweden thinks that I am a worthwhile human being? and not just a disposable slave?

The gift that the King of Sweden gave my mother to take back to her husband in Romania.

King of Sweden's Royal Monogram imprinted on the silverware

This picture is a simulation of what the silverware might have looked like

In her memoir, my mother blesses the people of Sweden for their generosity, goodwill, and kindness towards her and all the other "Flykling" refugees that were so incredibly surrounded by love and care in Sweden.

As a child, I clearly remember seeing the silver spoons with the king's stamp on them. My mother only let us use them on very special occasions. This was truly a meaningful and deeply sentimental gift for her. It reassured her that there were still noble, good-hearted, and generous people in this world.

We believe that Bracha might have sold some portion of that silverware set, to buy a ticket for her beloved sister Miriam, so she could also return to Romania.

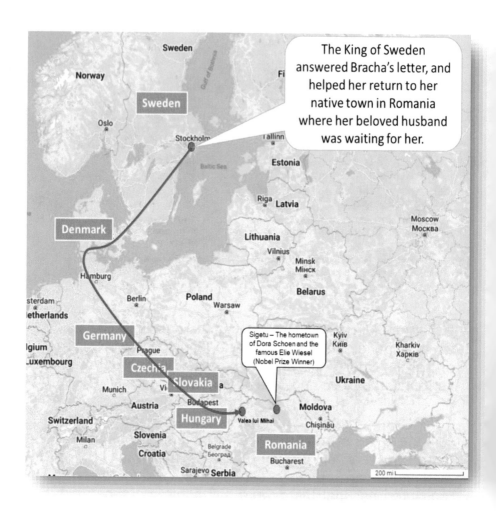

Map 4 – Return Home with the help from King of Sweden

Sadly, as our family left Romania to immigrate to the United States, the Swedish King's gift was confiscated by the Communist Romanian border guards - essentially stolen. During that time, the Communist Romanian government seized valuable possessions from Jews who were leaving for non-communist countries.

The communist regime confiscated homes, furniture, jewelry, watches, and even cut small earrings from little girls' ears. The special and memorable gift from the King of Sweden was forever lost due to the thievery of the Communist Romanian government.

With the train tickets in hand, my mother embarked on a 2700 km trip to get her back from Sweden to her native town in Romania.

She packed up her few belongings, along with the King's gift, and headed for the main train station in Stockholm, the Swedish capital. She was accompanied to the train station by her sister Miriam, her sisters-in-law Esther and Rifka, and many of her friends. With a heavy heart, she bid them farewell, with the hope and expectation that they would soon meet again back home.

From Sweden, the train journeyed through Denmark, Germany, Czechia, Slovakia, Hungary, and finally arriving in her native Romania. In this very long voyage, the reverse of her Holocaust journeys, she travelled in fancy Pulman train cars rather than in cattle cars.

After changing several trains, she finally arrived in her small Romanian hometown of Valea lui Mihai.

Bracha returned from Sweden in 1946 to her hometown in Romania.

Tzvi waited for his beloved wife at the train station in Romania.

Imagine the extraordinary, overwhelming joy she experienced upon once again seeing the face of her beloved husband, Tzvi (Herman), waiting for her at the train station. My father took her back to their old home, which had been ransacked by both soldiers and neighbors during the war.

Before my mother's arrival, my father somehow managed to re-furnish their little home with basic essential items such as chairs, a table, some dishes, and a bed. This was a remarkable achievement, considering that it was right after World War II when everything was in short supply and very expensive.

My mother was also elated to see her brother, Julius (Gyula), and her brothers-in-law, Moshe (Moric), Menyus, and Sam (Sanyi), who, miraculously, had also survived the Holocaust.

After the initial euphoria and excitement wore off, the bitterness over the loss of her two beautiful, innocent sons took hold of my mother. Everywhere she looked, she heard her murdered children's voices calling out to her, "Mommy, mommy .. help me."

The room where the children slept, the backyard where they played, the streets where they walked, everything reminded her of the unfathomable tragedy of losing her sons. When she stumbled upon a torn album, with photos of her sons' happy faces, she became totally overwhelmed. That pushed her into a deep depression, marked by uncontrollable crying episodes.

Call it post-traumatic stress disorder or call it survivor's guilt; the thought of, "Why did I survive while my children died," became an overwhelming and overpowering emotion. On many nights, she would wake up, walk onto the nearest train tracks, and pray that an approaching train would come and end her life, allowing her to re-unite with her sons in heaven.

An exceedingly kind, local doctor in town, Dr. Kozak, heard about my mother's depression and requested to see her. After talking with her, he recommended that the only way she could recover from this terrible tragic depression, would be to start a new family. She was still young enough to have healthy children and start a fresh chapter in her life.

Starting a new Life

Following the kind doctor's insightful recommendation, at age 36, she gave birth to her third son - me, the author of this book. Miraculously, along with my birth, was born a new sense of optimism, and a fierce determination to provide a bright, new future for her newfound family. From then on, the dark clouds faded, and a ray of sunshine was peeking through her life.

The beautiful, 34-year-old Bracha, back in her hometown of Valea lui Mihai, Romania.

She looks confident that she can start a new life and have a new family, despite the unspeakable tragedies she had suffered at the hand of the Nazi murderers.

With a new sense of purpose, and reason to live, she hoped for a better future for herself and her son. Then, a short year and a half later, she welcomed another son into the world—my brother, Joseph, who brought her immense joy and an additional sense of purpose. With the birth of my brother, she finally felt that God had returned to her the loving family that the Nazis so brutally had robbed from her.

Remarkably, she never talked about her tragic past, never displayed signs of distress or bitterness in the presence of her children, and consistently celebrated joyful events with a cheerful disposition. She had a beautiful voice, sang beautifully joyful melodies to us, enjoyed regular trips to the park, and took us to movies. She encouraged us to exercise our imaginations, make up games and build snowmen during the winter months.

1951 –

Bracha with her husband Tzvi and her two new sons, Tom and Joe.

To this day, I cannot fathom, or even begin to understand, how my mother was able to suppress her horrific past, commit herself fully and joyfully to her family, and be able to live a happy, normal life. She consistently radiated happiness and raised two happy children. Our own happiness mirrored the positivity she constantly projected. Alas, what she felt in the deepest recesses of her heart, we will never really know.

My mother lived with her family in her native village until her sister Miriam got married and moved to a larger city called Baia Mare. Then she wanted to be close to her sister, so she also moved with her family to the regional city of Baia Mare.

During this period, Romania became a satellite of the Soviet Union, and the entire country fell under the rule of a police state led by a communist dictator. Our whole family had to find a way to live within the constraints of a communist regime. This regime allowed no freedom of speech or religion, and all businesses were government owned. Consequently, there was no competition and prices for all items were fixed by government rules.

1962 – Bracha with her family, right before they emigrated from Romania.

From left to right

50-year-old Bracha,

14-year-old Joseph

53 year-old Tzvi

15-year-old Thomas

After 16 years of living in communist Romania, our family was finally able to get an exit visa to leave Romania. At that time, the Israeli government managed to bribe some high-ranking Romanian officials to allow a limited numbers of Jewish people to leave Romania[53].

---

[53] Opinion | RANSOM FOR ROMANIA'S JEWS - The Washington Post
https://www.washingtonpost.com/archive/opinions/1991/10/20/ransom-for-romanias-jews/803bf673-9557-4821-be79-5f81781bbcef/

Ransom of the Jews: The Story of the Extraordinary Secret Bargain Between Romania and Israel
https://www.amazon.com/Ransom-Jews-Extraordinary-Bargain-Between/dp/1566635624

/

Again, a Stateless Refugee

Our family was allowed to leave Romania with the condition that we leave all our valuable possessions behind and renounce our Romanian citizenship. The communist regime confiscated homes, furniture, jewelry, watches, and even cut small earrings from little girls' ears. This is how Romanian government robbed my mother of her precious silverware that she received from the King of Sweden.

Our family left Romania as stateless refugees, with the hope of finding a better future in a free country. With the assistance of the Jewish agencies (HaSochnut)[54], we were able to get to Vienna, Austria. After staying there for two weeks, the Jewish agency provided us the train tickets to get to Naples Italy where we were planning to take a ship to Israel.

While waiting to board a ship to Israel, my father's sister Esther[55] contacted us and advised to try and obtain an entry visa to the USA, with the option to come to Israel later. Esther sent my father $100 and asked him to contact the HIAS[56] in Rome for assistance. It so happened that my father had a brother (named Sam) living in New York who was willing to guarantee the family's passage to the USA.

---

[54] Jewish Agency for Israel - Wikipedia
https://en.wikipedia.org/wiki/Jewish_Agency_for_Israel

[55] Esther was the one was with my mother through the horrors of the Holocaust, but at this time she was living in Israel.

[56] HIAS is a Jewish American nonprofit organization that provides humanitarian aid and assistance to refugees worldwide.

With that in mind, my father traveled to Rome and with assistance from the HIAS agency, applied for entry visas to the USA. Since the process took some time, the HIAS agency sponsored our family to stay in the city of Genoa, Italy, until the USA visa was approved.

This was the time of the Cold War when a limited number of refugees from communist countries were allowed to immigrate legally to the USA. Each country had an immigration quota; for instance, those coming from communist Czechoslovakia had the lower quota than those coming from Romania.

Once again, my mother was living on charity, but this time the charity was temporary, and it had a hopeful ending to it. The Jewish agency provided a bedroom room for our family in an apartment shared by four families. The room was on the fourth floor with no elevators, and the one bathroom, and kitchen were shared by four families.

For my brother and me, being in Genoa was a true delight. The view from the fourth floor was magnificent and we had a great time socializing with the other teenagers in the apartment. We had enough food, we had a place to sleep, and we were free to explore the city on foot. We had no money, but we were free, and we were very content.

We decided to attend the local synagogue, which needed additional men to form a minyan (a quorum of 10 people) for prayer services. Knowing that we were refugees, they were willing to pay us for a bus fare so we could get to the synagogue on time. We got there on time, but we didn't take the bus. We walked, and we saved the bus fare.

After a few weeks of savings, we had enough money to attend a newly released movie. We watched for the first time a movie on a panoramic surround-screen with stereophonic sound. The movie was called "Cleopatra," starring the superstar Elizabeth Taylor in the leading role and I still vividly remember what an incredible treat and delight that was.

The local bakery needed help, and my brother and I decided to assist. For that we were allowed to bake challah, breads, and cakes there. We also befriended the baker's son, who gave us rides in his small Fiat car. He was a very kind person who was proud to show us all the beautiful spots on the Italian Riviera.

All dressed and ready to leave Genoa, Italy in 1964.

From left to right
16-year-old Joseph (my brother)
52-year-old Brocha (my mother)
55-year-old Tzvi (my father)
17-year-old Thomas (the author of this book)

As you can notice, the pants were a little short on both Joseph and me. As teenagers we grew a lot in the 10 months we spent in Italy waiting for our visa to enter the USA legally.

After ten months of living in a very humble but carefree, and peaceful environment, in June 1964 we finally got the visa to legally enter the USA.

Emigrating legally to the USA

From Genova, we boarded a ship called SS Independence which had about two hundred passengers on board. The ship appeared luxurious to us because it featured a swimming pool and a dining room where we enjoyed three meals a day, served by a waiter.

Our accommodation was a windowless room located at the bottom of the ship, equipped with two bunk beds that could accommodate the four of us. This room was situated adjacent to the engine room, which we humorously referred to as the "boom-boom room" due to the considerable noise from the running engine which kept us up most of the night.

The ship also carried many other refugee families like ours. My mother spent most of her time playing rummy with friends or simply enjoyed the fresh air as she walked around the ship with my father. This was a dream come true, because she dreamed of going on a cruise with her husband.

This is the passenger ship, with about 200 passengers, that took us from Genova, Italy across the stormy Atlantic Ocean to New York City, USA.

The passenger list shows the Goldstein family of four:
Mr. Herman (Tzvi- My father)
Mrs. (Brocha – My mother)
Mr. Toma H. (Thomas -the author of this book)
Mr. Josif (Joseph – my brother- The editor of this book)

List of Passengers
Tourist Class

⚓

S. S. Independence

SAILING FROM NAPLES
SUNDAY, JULY 12, 1964
to
GENOA, CANNES, ALGECIRAS AND NEW YORK

GENOA (cont'd)

Fernandez, Mr. Felix
Ferrari, Mr. Pietro
Ferrari, Mrs.
Ferrari, Mstr. Tiziano
Flaim, Mr. Stefano
Fulga, Miss Jean

Goldstein, Mr. Herman
Goldstein, Mrs.
Goldstein, Mr. Toma H.
Goldstein, Mr. Josif

Hinck, Miss Christina R.

Khoury, Mr. Nasim O.

Lerner, Mrs. Bella

Maffei, Mrs. Assunta T.
Martini, Mr. Eugenio
Mendelovici, Mr. Herz
Mendelovici, Mrs.

Pegoraro, Mr. Giorgio
Popligher, Mr. Josif
Popligher, Mrs.
Popligher, Mr. Mihail

Ravaglia, Mrs. Rita
Rosenberg, Mr. Isidor
Rosenberg, Mrs.
Rozsa, Mr. Adras

Scheiman, Mrs. Rozalia
Simonetti, Mr. Ivan

GENOA (cont'd)

Weisz, Mr. David
Weisz, Mrs.
Weisz, Miss Sara
Weisz, Miss Margareta
Weisz, Miss Viorica

Zupo, Mrs. Elza

EMBARKED at CANNES

Beraud, Mr. Jean M. A.

Masotti, Miss Vivien

EMBARKED at ALGECIRAS

Aurell Fayos, Mrs. Carmen
Aflalo, Mr. Charles

Baldwin, Mr. Harland S.
Baldwin, Mrs.
Baldwin, Mstr. Mark
Baldwin, Mstr. Johathan

Carandell, Mr. Juan
Carandel, Mrs.

Del Castillo, Mr. Enrique J.
Perez y Garay, Mrs. Miriam C.
Del Castillo Perez, Miss Myriam P.

Kent, Mr. John P.

The calm Mediterranean Sea gave way to stormy Atlantic Ocean once we sailed past the Straits of Gibraltar. Many passengers experienced seasickness, but the younger individuals, like my brother and me, had a great time playing ping-pong on the bouncing ship. The crew tried to entertain us and allowed us to go up to the tourist deck where there was a pool, and we could play basketball. They also taught us how to play shuffleboard and my brother Joe won the shuffleboard championship tournament. This was truly exciting since shuffleboard was a brand-new game for him.

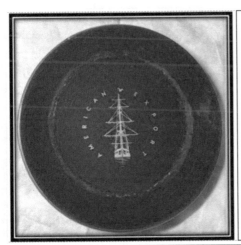

During a turbulent Atlantic crossing, my brother Joe emerged victorious in the shuffleboard championship tournament.

The challenging conditions added a unique twist to the game, as players had to synchronize their movements, and balance, with the ship's bouncing.

Joe's remarkable achievement earned him the shuffleboard trophy, accompanied by numerous congratulations from both passengers and crew members alike.

After ten days of sailing from Italy, crossing the Mediterranean Sea and the Atlantic Ocean, we finally reached the "Promised Land" and sailed into the New York Harbor. The first sight that greeted us was not the Statue of Liberty, but the recently completed majestic Verrazano Bridge.

We landed in New York city on my brother's 16ᵗʰ birthday. His birthday present was that he arrived safely in a free country where we could have a future with hard work. At the time we were so excited seeing New York City that we could not imagine what freedom meant. It took us many years to understand the responsibility and the opportunities that come along with becoming part of a free society.

In New York, with the assistance of the HIAS agency, we moved into a two-bedroom apartment in the Crown Heights section of Brooklyn.

As new immigrants, we've encountered economic struggles. Life was not a "Bowl of Cherries". We arrived with no resources, facing poverty and uncertainty. Employment opportunities were scarce. Especially for those lacking specialized skills or English proficiency. We took any job that was offered to us; from selling ice cream on the beach to day laborers in a hotel. My brother and I were enrolled in the local public high school but we both had to work after school to earn some money. We both worked as delivery boys for the local butcher and grocery store.

The lack of employment meant that we had to make do with very little income, making it difficult to afford basic necessities. After many months without employment my mother (since she was a skilled dressmaker), was lucky to find a job in a sweatshop in lower Manhattan. After many years at this job, she became disabled and lost her job. Disabled and in constant pain, my mother did not give up... even here in America. She opened an alteration shop right in her apartment.

My father accepted a job in a commercial kitchen as a cook's assistant. Later in life he found a job as a bookbinder, a job which he loved since this was his real profession.

Housing conditions were not the greatest either, but we managed. We lived in a fairly bad neighborhood on Albany Avenue in Brooklyn, NY. We furnished the apartment with used furniture and carpeting sometimes salvaged from the streets. We tried to create a semblance of a home with whatever we could find.

Despite these challenges we were very happy and felt grateful to be able to apply for US citizenship. We studied US History, US governance and the US constitution and finally, in front of a judge, we were sworn in as proud USA citizens. We were no longer stateless but were proud citizens of a free and strong country.

Once my mother was no longer a stateless refugee, she was able to travel abroad to visit her beloved sister, Miriam, in Israel.

Our parents were overjoyed that they finally found a new life in a free country with a promising future for their children. After several years, we relocated to Flatbush and later to the Borough Park section of Brooklyn to be closer to our family members.

My parents lived a very happy and productive life in the US and were able to attend their two sons' weddings. They witnessed the birth of their five grandchildren and my mother was even able to attend some of her grandchildren' weddings.

My mother became a very dedicated and skillful nurse to her husband Tzvi, who suffered from chronic heart disease. For over ten years, she cared for her ailing husband in a loving and devoted manner. At one point, my father's cardiologist, Dr. Fox, remarked that Bracha's efforts had extended her husband's life by an extra 10 years.

On May 21, 1995, (21st of Iyyar, 5755) Bracha lost her beloved 86 years old husband, and shortly afterward, she could no longer walk and was diagnosed with Parkinson's disease. She had to be moved from her Brooklyn apartment, and that is when we discovered her Holocaust Memoir, which is the subject of this book.

Bracha passed away on the 26th of February 1999 (10th of Adar, 5759) at the age of 87 after creating a new family with two sons, 5 grandchildren and 15 great grandchildren.

She was laid to rest next to her beloved husband in, Beth Israel Cemetery, Woodbridge NJ, USA –

Bracha and her husband Tzvi's Tombstone in Beth Israel Cemetery, Woodbridge, NJ, USA.

Notice that Bracha's headstone is leaning toward her husband's, as if she is trying to remain close to him, even in the cemetery.

Chapter 5 - Bracha blessed the Swedish Nation in her memoir, but why did she not curse the Nazis?

As I was translating my mother's memoir, I was puzzled by the fact that my mother refrained from cursing the vicious Nazi killers, who murdered her two beloved sons, her parents, her siblings, and turned them into ashes over the Polish countryside. It seemed only natural for her to bless the Swedish nation for helping her, but why did she refrain from cursing her tormentors, the Nazis?

Throughout my upbringing, I never heard my mother expressing any hatred toward the Germans. Now, considering what we have uncovered in her memoirs, I find myself at a loss to explain this. It's possible that she harbored a profound hatred but kept it buried deep inside, choosing not to openly express it. Perhaps she was so successful in projecting the image of a kind, loving mother, that she suppressed her own hatred, wanting her sons to grow up learning how to love rather than hate other people.

Years ago, when I was working as an engineer for a major corporation, my supervisor assigned me a significant task: to accompany our marketing team, serving as their technical expert, on a crucial trip to Germany.

I expressed my reluctance, citing the atrocities committed by the German people against my family and fellow Jews during World War II. I begged him to find someone else for the assignment. "You have been with this project since its inception, you are our most qualified expert," he insisted, "and your presence is crucial for us to be awarded this major government contract."

At that point, even though I was completely clueless about my mother's actual war-time experiences, I did explain to my boss that my mother was a Holocaust survivor. I offered a compromise to my boss. I told him that I would agree to go on the trip, only if my mother would approve my going to Germany.

When I spoke to my mother about the work-related trip to Germany, she didn't respond with a flat "No! You should never set foot on German soil!", or "Don't do business with murderous Germans." Instead, she simply said, "Just be careful and come home safely."

How can one explain that attitude in light of so much pain and horror?

I recently read a book called **The Choice**, by Dr. Edith Eger, who was also a Holocaust survivor. She argues that by harboring hatred, you put yourself in a mental prison. One should remember and honor the past, but that is quite different from remaining stuck in guilt, shame, and anger. Choosing hope and focusing on the positive can be liberating.

I do not believe that that my mother had forgiven the Nazis, but she had found a way to heal by instinctively deciding not to hate. Instead, she focused on loving and caring for her current family.

Maybe she also realized that not all Germans were complicit in the atrocities. Maybe she understood that the ultimate response to German evil was the complete defeat of Nazi Germany, the establishment of the Jewish State of Israel, and the successful upbringing of a new generation of Jewish children.

My mother's strength, resilience, and spirit were incredibly uplifting and emotionally inspiring.

It turns out that I did go to Germany, and our corporation succeeded in winning that significant government contract. I found that the Germans I encountered were truly kind and helpful, despite being aware of my Jewish identity. Holocaust studies were mandatory in German high schools, and teenage students were required to go on field trips to the German death camps and Holocaust memorials.

To underscore the shift in German attitudes, I met a 20-year-old German engineering student at a trade show who was well-versed in Holocaust history and had chosen to volunteer in an Israeli Kibbutz during his summer vacation.

Can one hate someone who demonstrates remorse and supports the Jewish people?

Chapter 6 – Early Life of Bracha (Bauer) Goldstein, the author of this Holocaust memoir?[57]

Bracha, was the third child in a poverty-stricken family of six siblings in the small village of Valea lui Mihai, Romania.[58]

Her father, (Victor Bauer), owned a horse and wagon which he used to transport merchandise from town to town. This occupation provided a very basic, meager income for his family of six children.

Like most young girls at that time and place, Bracha spent her childhood assisting her mother with household chores and helping care for her younger siblings. Because her mother was a very kind and loving person, Bracha grew up feeling enriched and fulfilled, despite their material poverty.

Then too, at that time and place, girls' education was not a priority, and young Bracha only received a bare, very basic education, learning to read and write in her native Hungarian language. Later, she also learned how to read Hebrew, enabling her to participate in Jewish prayer services.

---

[57] Her Holocaust memoir is shown in Chapter 1
[58] See Family Trees – Bracha's parents, siblings, and spouses.

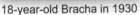
18-year-old Bracha in 1930   18-year-old Tzvi in 1928

Despite receiving such a very minimal education, her natural curiosity led her to borrow and voraciously devour books. Because books were very expensive, readers with modest means usually borrowed books from local bookstores for a fee, instead of buying books.

As fate would have it, one of Bracha's favorite bookstores was owned by the Goldstein family.In that very bookstore, she met and befriended Tzvi (Herman) Goldstein who was destined to become her husband.

Tzvi was not only a professional bookbinder, which at that time was a highly regarded profession, but also a very dashing, handsome, young man. He repaired and maintained all the books in his father's bookstore and delivered newspapers and other items for his father's business. In those days, providing books and newspapers was a lucrative business, because books and newspapers were the primary sources of information and entertainment.

The sparks of romance were kindled. Tzvi was naturally attracted to the pretty young girl who was so very fond of reading. He often gifted her with free books and newspapers. Somehow, Bracha's visits to the Goldstein bookstore only seemed to occur when Tzvi was present in the store. Slowly but surely, they fell in love and began a multi-year-long courtship. I discovered some very cute postcards that they wrote to each other during their lengthy courtship.[59]

Like many young Romanian men in the early 1930s, Tzvi was drafted and served in the Romanian army. Bracha waited very anxiously and apprehensively, for three long years, for him to return home.

1932
Picture of Tzvi in uniform, after being drafted into the Romanian military.

Meanwhile, Bracha's father experienced some serious financial problems because he often gambled, and many times had bad luck. Once, he took a risk and gambled with the merchandise on his cart that didn't belong to him. Unfortunately, he lost and had to pay for the merchandise,

---

[59] See Appendix C - for some cute examples of their correspondence during their long courtship.

but he didn't have the money. This could have landed him in debtor's prison, leaving his family of six children with no income.

Luckily, a wealthy Jewish family in town heard about the Bauer family's situation. They needed a housekeeper and nanny for their children and decided to hire Bracha and her sister Miriam. To help their father, the girls agreed to work for this family for three years, and in return, the family would pay off their father's debt. Bracha and Miriam were diligent workers, taking good care of the children and the household and the family really liked them.

To reward them for their dedicated work, the head of this family decided to provide a better future for the two girls. He sponsored Bracha and later Miriam to become apprentices to a dressmaker. This allowed Bracha to become a seamstress, which gave her a valuable lifelong profession.

By the time Tzvi finished his military service and was honorably discharged, Bracha was already working as a full-time seamstress, and was earning a good salary.

Bracha and Tzvi decided to get engaged and ask for their parents' consent to get married.

Bracha and Tzvi's engagement in January 1935

Initially, Tzvi Goldstein's parents objected to the proposed marriage because Bracha came from such a poor family. However, when they realized that their son was so much in love with Bracha, and that she was a bright, capable, young woman, who was earning a respectable living as a seamstress, they eventually consented.

In June 1935, Tzvi and Bracha got married and established a beautiful loving home, in the same little village of Valea lui Mihai, Romania.[60]

A year after they got married, Bracha had a beautiful healthy son named Istvanka (nicknamed Pityuka) and two years later they had another son named Tibi (nicknamed Tibike).

---

[60] See Appendix C for picture of Bracha and Tzvi's wedding and the identity of people who attended their wedding.

Bracha and her husband Tzvi lived happily and peacefully, raising their two children while enjoying a beautiful family life. Their brothers, sisters, and parents all lived within walking distance, in the same sleepy village.

This is a photo of Bracha's two sons before World War II.

Istvanka – (also nicknamed Pityuka) the older one (probably three years old in this picture) born in 1936.Tibike the younger one (about a year old in this picture) was born in 1938. Both of my two beautiful brothers, whom I never got to know, were murdered by the Germans in Auschwitz.

The 26-year-old Bracha (on the left) with her son Tibike and her 18-year-old sister-in-law Esther.

It looks like they were shopping and preparing for a cold season.

This photo was taken in 1938.

It is possible that they got dressed (I love those hats) and took the train to go shopping in the nearby city of Oradea.

There was not much shopping in their little town of Valea lui Mihai.

At that time the Jewish community comprised 20% of the population in Valea lui Mihai. [61] The town had a large synagogue, a Jewish school for boys, a mikveh (ritual bath)

61

See the Reference website for the Valea lui Mihai Jewish history at -
https://kehilalinks.jewishgen.org/valea_lui_mihai/

and a shochet (ritual butcher) who provided kosher meat for the community.

This seemingly idyllic life was suddenly uprooted when Nazi Germany occupied their section of Hungary in 1944. With the incomprehensible and enthusiastic cooperation of the local Hungarian fascist government, the deadly persecution of the Indigenous Jewish population commenced[62].

The entire Jewish population was deported to a ghetto in the nearby city of Oradea. From there, the Jews were systematically transported to death camps and slave labor camps in Poland and Germany.

---

[62] See Chapter 1

Chapter 7 - Miriam's story

Miriam was the youngest sister among her six siblings. She grew up in the little village of Valea lui Mihai, alongside her older sister Bracha.

Bracha and Miriam shared a close bond as sisters, becoming inseparable after their experiences during the Holocaust. In her memoir, Bracha frequently mentions her younger sister Miriam, whom she continually protected to ensure her survival amidst the horrors of the Holocaust. After their liberation and arrival in Sweden, Miriam recovered from tuberculosis in a special sanatorium where Bracha worked as a nurse's aide.

Following the end of the Second World War, Miriam returned to Romania where she met a young man named

Baruch Rooz, who resided in the city of Baia Mare. Baia Mare was a well-known mining town in Romania, and at that time, Baruch worked in the mines. Later, he became a manager at a small grocery store. Baruch and Miriam got married[63] and were blessed with two beautiful daughters: Ana in 1948 and Ella in 1951.

Miriam with her husband and two daughters around 1960.
From left to right:
9-year-old Ella,
44-year-old Miriam,
53-year-old Baruch
12-year-old Anna
Notice that Ella is the only one smiling. She was a happy child and grew up to be a happy adult who enjoyed singing and dancing.

Due to his work in the mines and heavy cigarette smoking, Baruch passed away from lung cancer on August 2, 1962

---

[63] See the Appendix C for Miriam and Baruch's 1947 wedding picture.

(2nd of Av, 5722) at the age of fifty-five. This left Miriam as a widow with two young children and very little income.

Miriam was struggling paying her bills and approached her sister with an intriguing proposition. "What do you think about renting out sleeping space in my apartment to temporary workers in town? I really need the extra income now that my husband is gone," Miriam proposed.

"You need to be cautious, though. You're alone with your two teenage daughters to look after," cautioned Brocha. "And your place only has a bedroom, a kitchen-dining area, and a bathroom. How would you manage sleeping arrangements?"

Miriam explained, "I plan to sleep in the bedroom with my daughters, and I can place two mattresses on the kitchen floor. They would only use the space for sleeping, not dining."

"There are some really kind people in town who just need a warm place to sleep during the cold winter months," she added.

"Alright, but please be careful and only accept trustworthy people," advised her sister.

Seeking to generate some income, Miriam proceeded with renting out sleeping space in her apartment to seasonal workers.

As fate would have it, a handsome young electrician named Jancu Leibel decided to rent a sleeping space from Miriam for several months. Jancu really liked being in Miriam's apartment and occasionally he even brought gifts for Miriam and her daughters.

Jancu got to know our family and became interested in dating Miriam's oldest 16-year-old daughter Anna. He even bribed my brother with a record player, to set up a date with Anna. Jancu and Anna dated for a while, and eventually fell in love with each other. They decided to get engaged with the promised to get married once they both emigrate to Israel.

Anna and Jancu engagement party.
We observe Miriam, the caring mother, embraced by her youngest daughter Ella, standing beside Anna, the bride.[64]

In 1964, Miriam and her two daughters were able to immigrate to Israel where Jancu was eagerly awaiting the arrival of his fiancé. Ana and Jancu were shortly married in Israel where they established a family and later had two sons.

---

[64] See Appendix C for the names of people on this picture.

In Israel, Miriam met a wonderful man named Jacob Rosenberg, whose family had tragically perished in the Holocaust. Since Jacob had no surviving family, he adopted Miriam's family and became a loving and caring father to Miriam's two daughters. He facilitated the exhumation of Miriam's first husband's (Baruch) remains from Romania and brought them to Israel so that the two daughters, Ana and Ella, could easily visit their father's grave.

Miriam's second daughter Ella also got married and established new families of her own with two daughters and two sons. Miriam's family tree now includes two children, six grandchildren, and 32 great-grandchildren.

Miriam passed away on 26th of July 1998 (3rd of Av,5758) at a good old age of 82. She was laid to rest in Ramla, Israel.

Jacob Rosenberg has been dearly loved and cared for by his two adopted daughters, who treated him as their real father. He lived a healthy and independent life for many years after Miriam's passing. When he reached the remarkable age of 100, his adopted family organized a grand birthday celebration attended by numerous friends and Miriam's entire family. Jacob eventually passed away at the age of 103. He was laid to rest not far from his beloved wife Miriam.

Baruch Rooz tombstone.
He died and was buried initially in Romania. Later, Jacob Rosenberg (Miriam's second husband) made the arrangement, and his remains were exhumed and reburied in Israel.

Miriam's tombstone in Ramla, Israel.

Jacob Rosenberg's (Miriam's second husband) tombstone in Ramla, Israel.

Chapter 8 - Esther's story

Esther was the eldest daughter in a family of nine children[65]. She grew up assisting her mother and learning the various tasks required to manage a household.

Esther Goldstein as a young woman full of life as she took on the role of caring for her younger siblings after her mother passed away.

Meanwhile, her father and older brothers were occupied with running a book, newspaper, and tobacco store in the small town of Valea lui Mihai, Romania.

---

[65] Based on interviews with Rachel (Fairfield) Mizrachi, Miram (Fuchs) Kagan and other family members.

In 1938, tragedy struck when Esther's mother was bitten by a cat that had rabies,[66] which led to her premature death. This left nine children orphaned.

After her mother passed away, Esther (at age 18), took on her mother's role of running the household and caring for her younger siblings. As the persecution of the Jews started in their town, Esther moved into her married brother's home (Tzvi's house) for comfort and safety. Bracha's memoir states that Esther, Rivka, and their father (Yehuda Leib) were arrested from her home by the Hungarian Gendarmes (armed police) and taken to the ghetto in Oradea and from there to the death camp of Auschwitz, in Poland. In Auschwitz Esther had **A10264** tattooed on her left arm.

Esther and Bracha experienced the horrors of the Holocaust together and their stories are vividly detailed in Bracha's memoir[67].

After their liberation, Esther appeared as a mere skeleton, weighing only 33kg (73lb). She was taken to Sweden under the care of the Red Cross, where she made a remarkable recovery and even secured factory work.

---

[66] Rabies is a viral infection that attacks the brain and is fatal if not treated immediately. In those days there was no vaccine or treatment for rabies, and it was always a deadly disease.

[67] See chapter 1 – Bracha's Memoir

1946

Esther on the right
with her sister Rivka
on the left,
recovering in
Sweden.

Picture was taken in
1946

During her nearly two-year stay in Sweden, Esther discovered the young Zionist movement. With support from the Haganah [68], this movement aimed to smuggle Holocaust survivors into the historical land of Israel, then under British mandate as Palestine.[69].

---

[68] Haganah was an underground Jewish organization in the British mandate of Palestine fighting for the establishment of a Jewish state.
https://www.jewishvirtuallibrary.org/the-haganah

[69] https://www.timesofisrael.com/the-secret-maritime-route-that-brought-holocaust-survivors-to-pre-state-israel/

Esther in Sweden (1946) as she was getting ready for a new life in the ancient land of Israel, which at the time was the British Mandate of Palestine.

Look at the glow in her face that expresses the hope and the belief she can create a better future for herself in the ancient land of Israel.

Esther with her sister Rivka, and numerous other Holocaust survivors boarded a cargo ship secretly bound for the British Mandate of Palestine. As they approached Palestine, their ship was intercepted by the British Navy, which compelled their vessel to change course and dock in the Mediterranean island of Cyprus. Here, all the passengers were placed in detention camps.

For most of those survivors interned in Cyprus, the experience only served to bolster their determination to reach the historic land of Israel. Most of them were able to achieve this goal following the establishment of the state of Israel in May 1948.

During her internment in Cyprus, Esther encountered a kind young man named Sanyi (Shmuel) Stauber. Esther and Shmuel fell in love and got married while they were in the Cyprus internment camp. They had a small wedding ceremony in 1948 officiated by a British military rabbi. The small wedding was attended by Ester's sister and a handful of friends.

There were many such weddings in Cyprus at that time because everyone was looking to start a new life and find a new home. It was reported that among the 70,000 people interned in the British Cyprus camps there were 2000 babies born between 1946 to 1948. After the establishment of the state of Israel in 1948, most Cyprus detainees were allowed to enter the newly established state of Israel. [70]

Esther and her husband Sanyi Stauber in the British detention camp in Cyprus

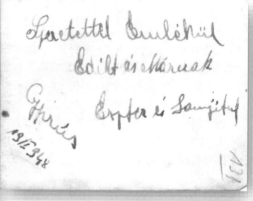

The back of the picture says in Hungarian:

With all our love memories to Edith and Moric (Esther's Brother and sister-in-law)

Cyprus   - January 19, 1948

---

[70]   See References – Cyprus Detention Camps

Following the establishment of the state of Israel, Esther and Shmuel emigrated to Israel where they established residency in the city of Haifa. There, they opened a pastry shop and both dedicated long hours to running a successful business.

Esther with her husband Shmuel in front of their pastry shop in Haifa in 1968

As their business became successful, they extended their support to siblings in Israel and even to those, living in communist Romania.

In 1959

Esther and her husband Smuel in their apartment in Haifa, Israel

Trying to adopt my sister's baby

Esther found contentment and happiness in Israel, except for the fact that she could not have any children due of the trauma and physical abuse she suffered during the Holocaust.

In the meantime, her sister Rivka got married and had two beautiful children. She often visited Esther's pastry shop where the children found a loving auntie, and lots of delicious pastries. Esther loved having the children in her shop but privately she expressed her frustration at not having her own children.

Rivka could not bear her sister suffering over childlessness and when she became pregnant with her third child she visited Ester.

"Give me a Mazel Tov" said Rivka "I am expecting my third child" "Wow – that is very exciting news – wishing you all the very best" responded Ester.

"I was thinking" continued Rifka "Since you do not have any children I would like to give you this baby. You could adopt it and raise it as your own. Thank God I already have two beautiful children and quite frankly we cannot afford additional expenses".

Ester's face lit up with excitement. "Are you sure? do you really mean to let me adopt your new baby?" "Yes – I see your suffering and beside my baby could not have a better, a more loving and caring mother than you."

Esther was overjoyed at the prospect of adopting her sister's baby.

She immediately went home and began preparing a room for the arrival of her adopted child. She purchased a crib, baby clothing, and eagerly awaited the arrival of her sister's baby. She regularly visited her sister to ensure that she received proper nutrition and prenatal medical care.

In the spring of 1955, a healthy and incredibly adorable baby boy finally arrived. Esther eagerly awaited this moment in the hospital and was overwhelmed with excitement when she could finally be able to cradle the cute baby boy in her arms. She had dreamt of this moment when she could welcome her sister's baby into her lovingly prepared home.

Beautiful 35-year-old Esther in Israel in 1955.

She was unable to have any children of her own because of the trauma and physical abuse she suffered during the Holocaust.

She was hoping to adopt and raise one of her sister's babies.

Rifka took the baby home and began nursing and caring for him, but she still intended to fulfill her promise to her sister. Then, the time for the Brit Milah (circumcision) arrived, and the baby was given the name Arye.

Ester was ecstatic that she would finally have a son. Not only that, but his future son was named after her late father who was murdered during the Holocaust. Her dream finally came true.

Then something totally unexpected happened. The baby's father, Joseph, decided that he couldn't part with his son. Even though they were strapped financially, he decided to work longer hours to earn more money, but he would not give up his son for adoption. Not even to his wife's sister!

Esther was devastated and ran home in tears. She was so hurt that she refused to see or speak to her beloved sister for six months. Over time, the rift between the two sisters healed. Esther gave the crib and all the baby clothing to Rivka, and they once again became good, loving sisters.

Esther had another sister, Frida, who also lived in Israel. Frida had managed to hide during World War II and did not endure the horrors of the death camps like Esther. After the war, Frida got married and emigrated to Israel, where she established a home and had three children: Moshe, Tzvia, and Atara.

Frida maintained a close relationship with her sister Esther and visited frequently Ester's pastry shop with her children. These visits offered a chance for the sisters to catch up, while the children reveled in the shop's abundant sweets. One day, Frida arrived alone and requested a private conversation with her sister.

"Ester," Frida began solemnly, "I just found out that I'm pregnant again. With three children already, money is tight. Raising another child feels impossible. Since the pregnancy is early, I'm considering an abortion."

Ester's eyes widened. "Oh no, Frida, please don't! for God's sake don't let finances be the reason. I'll support you throughout the pregnancy, and even... I'd be honored to adopt the baby and raise it with love and care as my own." Her voice trembled, "Please, Frida, reconsider."

"Okay, Ester," Frida said, her voice thick with emotion. "I love you dearly, and I want you to have a child too. I won't go through with the abortion. I'll carry this baby to term so you can have a healthy child of your own."

Ester was ecstatic at the possibility of becoming a mother to her sister's baby. Every week, she made the trip from Haifa to Lod to visit Frida and ensure she had everything she needed for a healthy delivery. This time, however, Ester exercised caution. She refrained from setting up a nursery with a crib or buying baby clothes in advance. Instead, she opted to wait until the baby was safely home with her before making any extravagant purchases.

Finally, in 1957, the joyous day arrived. Frida delivered a beautiful, healthy baby girl. The infant seemed to radiate happiness, smiling from the moment she was placed beside her mother. An early, genuine smile on a newborn was rare and truly remarkable. The baby's infectious joy spread through the room, creating an atmosphere of profound happiness.

They named the baby Rachel. However, Frida found herself unable to part with the radiant, smiling child. It wasn't the father, but Frida herself who clung stubbornly to her precious daughter and refused to give her up for adoption to her sister.

Tzvia	Frida	Eliezer	Moshe
(8 years)	(35 years)	(41 years)	(13 years)
Atara		Rachel (4 years) –	
(6 years)		Ester saved her and later was trying to adopt her as a baby	

Ester's sister Frida and her family in 1961

Poor Esther, though disappointed, wasn't crushed like before. Instead, she focused on showering Frida's children with love. She visited frequently, bringing them toys and clothes. Esther even invited them to spend their summer vacations at her delightful pastry shop, treating them like family. In essence, Esther became a second mother, not just to one, but to all four of Frida's children.

In 1985, Esther suffered the loss of her beloved husband Shmuel.

Then, in 1993, she faced another sorrow as her younger sister Frida passed away.

The proud and beautiful Esther looks very confident in this picture taken in 1961.

She should be proud that she was among the early pioneers who arrived and helped built the infant country of Israel.

She helped raise her sister's four lovely children because she could not have a natural child of her own.

For 17 years, she lived as a widow, finding solace in the company of Frida's children, her adopted family. Esther relocated from her Haifa apartment to a place closer to her adopted family in Tel Aviv. Frida's children, who had become her own, provided the love, comfort, and care that one would only expect from natural children at old age.

After all, Esther succeeded in having her own loving and caring family.

Esther passed away on July 7th, 2002 (24th of Tamuz, 5762) at the ripe age of 82 and she was buried in Israel.

Chapter 9 - Rivka's story

Rivka (Regina) Goldstein

as a young woman

around 1940

Rivka [71] was born on November 24, 1924, in the small town of Valea lui Mihai, in Romania. She was only 14 years old when her mother was bitten by a cat that had the deadly rabies virus. Sadly, her mother passed away in 1938, leaving behind nine orphaned children, with the youngest, Frida, being around 11 years old. Following their mother's death, Rivka, along with her older sister Esther, took on the responsibility of managing the bustling household.

Poverty and the upheavals of World War II deprived Rivka of the opportunity for any formal education. This resulted in difficulties with her reading and writing and left her

---

[71] Based on interview with Rivka's daughter - Miriam Kagan- and other family members.

feeling insecure and inferior. She relied on her older siblings to explain things that she could not comprehend.

Then in 1944, along with all the other Jewish residents of her town, Rivka was forcibly taken to the Ghetto in Oradea, and from there, transported in cattle cars to the death camp in Auschwitz, Poland. In Auschwitz, the Germans assigned her a new name, **A10265**, tattooed on her left arm.

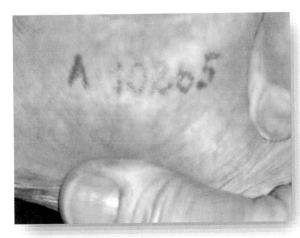

Rivka's left arm tattoo when she was already 80 years old.

This horrific tattoo was a lifetime reminder of her tragedy during the

Holocaust

During the Holocaust period, Rivka's experiences closely mirrored those documented by Bracha's memoir[72]. At the outset of her Holocaust experience, Rivka was an unmarried 20-year-old young woman in good physical shape. This played a crucial role in her survival amidst the tortures and suffering inflicted by the Germans.

After enduring the horrors of the Holocaust, Rivka found herself in terrible mental and physical shape, weighing

---

[72] See Chapter 1 where Bracha's tells their Holocaust story.

only 38 kg (84 lb). Thanks to the assistance of the Red Cross, she was transported to Sweden, where she received proper nourishment, clothing, and medical care.

Under the care of the Red Cross for several months, Rivka gradually recovered and secured employment at a local factory. This provided her with a modest income, enabling her to travel to the nearby capital city of Stockholm. The journey to the bustling Swedish capital held a certain magic for her, considering that she came from a small, dusty Romanian town. The visit to the big city of Stockholm is described in Bracha's memoir as a peaceful and tranquil place where they were surrounded by loving people and not by hateful Nazis.

Rivka spent nearly two years in Sweden, contemplating her uncertain future. When her sister-in-law, Bracha, returned to Romania, Rivka and her sister Esther made the decision to embark on a journey to the ancient land of Israel.

Rifka, along with her sister Esther, boarded a ship bound for Palestine, with the assistance of a Jewish Zionist organization known as the Haganah. Their hope was to find a home in the ancient land of Israel, which at that time was the British mandate of Palestine[73]. As they were sailing in the western Mediterranean Sea, their boat was intercepted by the British Navy, and all the holocaust survivors were taken to a detention camp in Cyprus[74].

In the Cyprus internment camp, Rivka endured almost two years of uncertainty and hardship. While the British internment camps provided food and shelter, they were

---

[73] https://www.timesofisrael.com/the-secret-maritime-route-that-brought-holocaust-survivors-to-pre-state-israel/

[74] See References – Cyprus Detention Camps

still prisons, with guards overseeing movement and strict rules that had to be followed. Despite the constraints, prisoners were allowed to socialize and participate in programs for training and acquiring new skills, such as operating sewing machines.

Rivka found joy when she learned of her sister Esther's plans to marry a wonderful man she had met in Cyprus. Rivka, along with some friends, organized a small celebration, and a military Jewish chaplain conducted the wedding ceremony. It was one of the happiest moments in Rivka's life, witnessing her beloved older sister get married under the chuppah[75]. This gave her hope that her life might eventually return to some semblance of normalcy after many agonizing years. She hoped that one of these days she would also find a husband and have a family of her own.

In 1948, the British government finally lifted its naval blockade and with the UN partition of Palestine, the independent state of Israel was established. Israel's Arab neighbors immediately attacked the young state of Israel and the Jewish state had to fight for its survival. Meanwhile, Rivka and her sister Esther were waiting anxiously in Cyprus listening to the news about Israel. Finally, after the Israeli victory they were transported from Cyprus to the port of Haifa in Israel. They arrived full of hope in an infant war-ravaged country with the knowledge that they finally were free and in a land of their own.

They faced a lot of challenges in a newly formed country that had very little to offer in terms of help for the new arrivals. Each new emigrant had to find their own niche in this very diverse and complex environment. Full of optimism, they all decided to rebuild their lives.

---

[75] Chuppah is the traditional Jewish wedding canopy.

Esther made earnest efforts to find a suitable husband for her sister, Rivka. She introduced Rivka to several young men, including her husband's brother, but none of these connections resulted in a successful match. However, Rivka's path to love took a turn when she met Joseph Fuchs, whom she married in 1951. Joseph Fuchs, born in Czechoslovakia in 1913, was older than Rivka, but he was an established businessman. Together with his brother Shmuel, he owned a bakery that supplied fresh bread to numerous local stores in Haifa.

HAIFA 1950

The beautiful 26-year-old Rivka in 1950, after she arrived in the newly established State of Israel.

Her sister Esther was trying to find a husband for her.

Finally, she found Joseph Fuchs, whom Rivka married in 1951.

Rivka and Joseph took up residence in a modest apartment situated in one of Haifa's suburbs, known as Kiryat Shmuel. In this new home, Rivka created a wonderfully clean and inviting environment. Their happiness was further enhanced when, in 1953, they welcomed their daughter, Miriam, into the world.

The 5-year-old Miriam

Full of life and carefree, enjoying growing up in a Kiryat Shmuel (a suburb of the city of Haifa, Israel)

Rivka experienced immense happiness in having a new family of her own. This allowed her to channel all her energy towards her family's future, freeing herself from the haunting memories of the Holocaust.

A few years later, Rivka welcomed two more children into her life: a son named Avrumi, affectionately nicknamed Yumi, and later, another son named Arye[76]. Rivka excelled as a fantastic homemaker and a loving mother to her three delightful children.

---

[76] Arye was almost adopted by Rivka's sister Esther. See Esther's story in Chapter 8.

Picture of Rivka's children around 1960.

Arye on the left

Miriam in the middle

Avrumi on the right

Her husband favored simple, everyday meals: fish, chicken with noodles, and other unfussy dishes. She, however, always catered to his preferences. Whenever she cooked fish, the aroma filled the house, prompting complaints from Miriam, Avrumi, and Arye. Unlike their father, the children weren't fans of the strong smell. Rivka would try to persuade them with a gentle scolding, "Freshly prepared fish is healthy and very nutritious!" Unfortunately, her pleas had little effect, and the children remained wary of anything fishy.

Rivka's husband, Joseph, worked long hours at the bakery to support their growing family. Over time, he developed a severe allergy to the flour used in breadmaking, which ultimately prevented him from continuing his work at the bakery. This situation prompted Joseph to explore the possibility of relocating with his family to the United States, where he had a brother in Cleveland and a cousin in Brooklyn who promised to assist him in finding a new job and establishing a fresh start in America.

The Fuchs family arrived in New York in 1961 with initial plans to settle in Cleveland near Joseph's brother. However, Joseph's cousin met them at the airport and convinced them to stay in Brooklyn, citing a more favorable environment for their children's education. The Fuchs family secured an apartment in the Crown Heights section of Brooklyn, where Joseph found work as a carpenter and assisted in his cousin's bakery. Joseph Fuchs was a very enterprising and hard-working person and he managed to save enough money to buy a 2-family house in the Canarsie section of Brooklyn. They rented out the top apartment and he even finished the basement which became another small apartment.

Rivka's children grew up in Brooklyn and after finishing their Yeshiva High School education they moved to different parts of the country. Miriam got married and moved to Detroit, Michigan, and Arye moved to Florida where he started a glass repair and installation business.

On the other hand, Avrum (Yumi) chose to remain in Brooklyn and reside in Rivka's basement apartment. Rivka was thrilled to have her son living under the same roof and took care to prepare his favorite foods, serving him a nourishing breakfast every morning.

One fateful morning in 1993, Avrumi didn't come for breakfast as usual. Rivka initially assumed he was simply sleeping late due to fatigue. Eventually, she decided to check the basement apartment and discovered to her horror that Avrumi was lying unconscious on the floor. She immediately called an ambulance, but sadly, her 39-year-old son was pronounced dead in the hospital due to a brain aneurysm.

Rivka was plunged into a state of shock, having endured the horrors of the Holocaust only to lose her beloved son in her own home. The Holocaust had been a collective national tragedy, but this loss was intensely personal and painful. Witnessing her son's death in her own home, left an unbearable burden that would haunt her for the rest of her life.

Avrumi was laid to rest in Woodbridge, New Jersey, at Beth Israel Cemetery, where Rivka and many other family members would eventually also find their final resting places.

Rivka's youngest son, Arye, resided in Florida and visited his mother whenever he had the opportunity. On one visit, she was visiting his brother's grave, he decided to invest $10,000 in purchasing six graves. He anticipated that these plots would be used to bury his mother and other older family members near the location where his brother Avrumi was also buried. Little did he know that he would be the first one to occupy one of those graves.

In 2010, the family received the tragic news from Florida, that Arye had suffered a massive heart attack and passed away at the age of fifty-five. They chose to keep this information from Rivka, who was already frail and was still mourning the loss of her older son. Fortunately, Arye had a close Lubavitch friend who arranged a proper burial ceremony and facilitated the transportation of his body to New Jersey. Arye was buried in the first grave of the cluster of six that he purchased earlier for the older family members in Woodbridge cemetery.

Rivka's daughter, Miriam, never disclosed Arye's death to her mother. She always found excuses for why Arye couldn't call anymore. "Why isn't Arye calling or visiting me anymore?" ask Rivka. "You know there were many hurricanes in Florida and Arye is busy replacing all the broken windows" her daughter would replay in a very strained voice. "Besides, he called many times - mom. The long-distance connection to Florida is terrible and you're hearing is so bad that you can't hear him talk over the telephone."

This way Rivka never found out that she lost not just one, but both of her sons prematurely.

Rivka passed away two years later, on January 1st, 2012 (6th of Tevet, 5772) at the age of eighty-eight. She was buried right next to her son Arye in the grave cluster that Arye purchased for the family in Beth Israel Cemetery, Woodbridge, New Jersey.

Rivka's tombstone

She passed away at the age of 88 and is buried next to her beloved son Arye in Woodbridge, NJ.

Chapter 10 - Dora Schoen –

- Dora grew up in the same town as the famous Nobel Prize winner Elie Wiesel.
- She typed my mother's memoir, and she was with her in German Concentration Camps and in Sweden.

I had the unique privilege of meeting Dora Schoen through her brother, Kalman Bash, whom I knew from Romania.

Kalman attended the same synagogue as I did in Highland Park, NJ. Dora lived very close to us, and on numerous occasions, she joined us for Shabbat or holiday meals and celebrations.

Dora could not have children of her own due to the horrific suffering and torture she endured in the German concentration camps. She was immensely grateful for the opportunity to spend time with and celebrate holidays alongside our children.

Dora was an exceptionally kind and compassionate woman. Along with her husband Eddie, she actively participated in various charitable organizations, including visiting on a regular basis patient in local hospitals.

Dora at my daughter's Bat Mitza in 1993

Back in Romania, Dora worked as a legal secretary and was the person responsible for transcribing and typing my mother's Hungarian handwritten memoir.

It's likely that while typing the memoir, Dora may have also made some editorial adjustments, perhaps inquiring about my mother's feelings regarding certain events recounted in the memoir. The memoir not only documents the factual aspects of the story but also delves into the emotions and sentiments experienced during those events.

Additionally, Dora played a pivotal role in assisting my mother in composing a letter addressed to the King of Sweden. In this letter, my mother sought the King's assistance in reuniting with her beloved husband in Romania.[77]

---

[77] See Chapter 4- Rest of Bracha's Story - Bracha got back home with help from the King of Sweden (story told by Dora Shoen).

Dora Shoen's video interview

Dora's interview by the Holocaust Resource Center at Kean University can be found at the link

https://collections.ushmm.org/search/catalog/irn507848

The Jewish history of the town of Sighet, where Dora Schoen and Nobel Prize winner Elie Wiesel were born, is depicted in the link provided below:

https://encyclopedia.ushmm.org/content/en/article/sighet

Oral History | Accession Number: 1993.A.0088.97 | RG Number: RG-50.002.0097

Dora Schoen (née Basch), born on July 10, 1919, in Sighet, Romania, describes her family and childhood; She was one of six children, including Abraham (b. 1906), Kalman (b. 1909), Roze (b. 1910), brother (b. 1913), and Zelda (b. 1921);

The main points of Dora's history as documented in the above Oral History Interview in 1993

- Her father was a butcher, and her mother helped in the butcher shop.
- Dora worked as a secretary in a lawyer's office until the Hungarian occupation of Transylvania at the end of August 1940.
- Jewish lawyers no longer were allowed to practice after the German invasion on March 19, 1944.
- The Hungarian Police placed all Jews in ghettos within Sighet in April 1944.

- They confiscated (robbed) of all the jewelry from the Jews and told them that they are being taken to Hungary to work on farms.
- They were put into cattle trains and taken to the Auschwitz death camp on May 14, 1944.
- Dora was separated from her family and never saw them again, except for the one sister Zelda and her brother Kalman.
- They all went through the selection process. She was given **a tattoo number A7606** and was placed in a working barrack.
- Dora spent two months in Beendorf salt mines working in an underground ammunition factory[78].
- She was liberated by the Red Cross at the Danish border where she was quarantined.
- She was transported to Landskrona, Sweden[79]. The Swedish people were very kind and brought them clothes.
- She had an aunt in the United States who sent her money and her surviving brother's address (he had been in Paris at the time of the German occupation)
- Dora's brother Kalman and sister Zelda returned to their home in Sighet, Romania[80] but she remained in Sweden for three more years and worked as a house mother for 40 people and in a clothing factory.
- She received a letter in 1946 from Edward Schoen who was a distant relative, who was in Palestine after the war.
- She was able to get to Palestine and married Edward at the end of April 1948, five days before Israel's Independence.

---

[78] See References – Nazi Underground Factories
[79] Dora was in this Swedish Town with my mother Bracha.
[80] Sighet (Sighetu Marmatiei) is also the Romanian town where the famous Nobel Prize winner Elie Wiesel was born.

- They lived in Israel for eight years (1948-1956)
- She was unable to have children because of the suffering she endured during the Holocaust.
- They decided to immigrate to the United States to live near her sister Zelda and her brother Kalman in Highland Park, New Jersey.

Appendix A –

First Page of Bracha's Original Memoir

Written in Hungarian, this memoir was transcribed and typed by Dora Schoen during their recovery in Sweden. Typed on legal-sized paper, it remained hidden in my mother's linen closet in her Brooklyn apartment. It was discovered only when she became ill and had to be moved out of her apartment.

The original manuscript now resides in the historical archive of Yad Vashem in Jerusalem, Israel, where it is preserved in humidity and temperature-controlled environment.

Remarkably, blue tear stains mark not only this page but also numerous other pages within my mother's memoir.

Egy szerencsétlen anya élettragédiája 1944-től 1945-ig.

1945.6.29:Svedország.Landskronai tüdőszanatorium.Most itt vagyok a dr
hugom betegágyánál.Nagyon nagy fájdalommal ujult fel bennem az elmult idő tör-
ténete.Megprobálom sorokba foglalni e szörnyü tragédiát.
1943-ig boldogan éltünk.drága jo férjemmel.Ekkor be kellett neki vonu
munkaszolgálatra Nagybányára.Én Érmihályfalván laktam nagyon megelégedetten ki
otthonomban.Két gyönyörü egészséges kisfiammal.Gyermekeim évkora egyik nyolc ma
sik hat éves.Nagyon boldog napjaink voltak amig férjem odahaza volt.Férjem bev
mulása összeroppant minden.Itt kezdődött életem tragédiája.
1944 március.Beköszöntött a tavasz s hozta magával a sok nyomoruságot,
szenvedést mely nem akart végeterni.Marcius 19.Villámcsapásként terjedt el a h
hogy a horogkeres ztes németek Europa rémei megszállták Magyarországot.Zürzav
felfordulások,minden rend felbomlott,s minden jozan gondolkodásnak vége.Az em-
berek s főleg mi szerencsétlen zsidok jajveszékelve tanácskoztunk egymás között
Jaj Istenem mi lesz velünk? Csak Istenem őrizzen a németek ki ne adjanak olyan
rendeleteket ami élőpéldákként állott előttünk Lengyelország,Szlovákia és többi
kis államok zsidóságának szomoru sorsa.ahova a németek betették veszedelmes lá
kat.Igen és eljött a szomoru valoság.Az ég beborult fejünk fölött a vihar hama
san közeledett.Vihar mely családfákat döntött ki gyökerestől s amelynek sok sol
ezer halálos áldozata lett.A rádio,magyar ujságok tele voltak zsidoellenes pro-
pagandával.Az első németek által kiadott rendelet a hatágu csillag köteles vise
lete volt,mely szigoruan megköveteli,hogy április 5től hat éven felüliek és
70 éves korig minden egyes zsido személynek kötelező a felső ruha balmellén a
sárga csillag viselése.Április 6.Már messziről viritottak a ruhára tüzött szé-
gyenfoltnak nevező csillagok s ez minnél jobban viritott annál sötétebben ált
előttünk a jövőnk.Pontos dátumra visszaemlékezni nem tudok,talán április 8.
Ujabb rendelet.Nagy plakátokkal minden házfalán hirdették,hogy zsidok semmifél
járművén nem utazhatnak.Másnap ujabb rendelet.Most már egyáltalán el sem hagyh
ja a lakását.Aki a parancsnak ellenszegül,az rögtön büntetőbiróság elé került,
amikor is oly nagy kinzásokat hajtottak végre rajtuk,amit leirni nem lehet.A
börtön s rendőrség fogdái állandoan zsufolva voltak ártatlan bünösökkel.mert
hogy a gyilkosok kezére jussanak elég volt az a bün,ha a sárga csillag nem volt
elég erősen révarrva ruhájukra.Április közepe felé ujabb plakátok,ujabb rendele
Zsido üzletek egyáltalán nem tarthatnak nyitva s egyben szigoruan megkövetelik
a zsidó magántulajdonok,vagyonok és értéktárgyak beszolgáltatását.S mivel a né
tek nem sokaig teketoriáznak,igy a rendeletet tettek követték.Mindenki nagyon
volt keseredve.drága jo szüleim és testvéreim,kik velem egy városban laktak,ki
ket ugy szerettem mint saját életemet.szeretett drága jo Édesanyám nagyon s
sirt,ő már látta mi fog történni és nagyon sötétnek látta gyermekei jövőjet.Fő
leg amikor megkezdődött a zsidok elhurcolása és kiüritése Máramarosbol.Ekkor
meg nem tudtuk mi az a szo getto.Éjjel nappal jöttek a tehervonatok melyek meg
kinzott zsido testvéreinket szállitották:Hova azt csak később tudtuk meg.Ér-
mihályfalván nagy pánik lett.Lopva,félve,tömegesen szaladtunk abban az időben
az állomáshoz,amikor szerencsétlen zsido testvéreink érkezését jelentették.Mindenk
szaladt megrakott kosarakkaltele élelmiszerrel,hogy segitsünk szegény szeren-
csétleneken.A kegyeteln felszuronyozott csendörök kéjmosollyal,megelégedéssel
nézték a tömegesen szerencsétlenül megérkezetteket s minden egyes alkalommal
puskatussal és gummibotokkal verték szét a tömeget.Vegül mindenki kisirt szem-
mel tántorgott hazafelé.A vonat elrobogott és vitte magával áldozatait.Később
kiderült,hogy szegény testvéreinket Mátészalkára telepitették le egy pusztára,
a szabad ég alá.A zsidóság jajveszékelt.saját sorsunkat láttuk az övékben.Egé

Yad Vashem has the Original Memoir

These are the letters documenting that my mother's original memoir is now in the Yad Vashem Archive under the registration mark 12203 and document number 0.33/4620

YAD VASHEM יד ושם

The Holocaust Martyrs' and Heroes' Remembrance Authority רשות הזיכרון לשואה ולגבורה

Mr. Joseph Goldstein

Jerusalem
November 12, 1995.

Dear Mr. Goldstein:

I acknowledge receipt of the facsimile Holocaust memoirs, written by Goldstein Hermanne in Malmo, Sweden.

The above-mentioned was registered at the Archives and may be referred to as No 12203.

As far as I could follow up, you are ready to donate to our Archives the original of the memoirs, which we appreciate in advance.

Sincerely,

Mark Shraberman
Acquisitions

81

YAD VASHEM   יד ושם

The Holocaust Martyrs' and Heroes' Remembrance Authority   רשות הזיכרון לשואה ולגבורה

Jerusalem
November 7, 1996.

]

U.S.A.

Dear Mr. Goldstein,

Your messenger David Hacham was really prompt enough to run your errand.

You were kind enough to keep your promise, and, therefore, we are in receipt of the original of Hermanne Goldstein's Holocaust memoirs.

You should call the document up in the future as 0.33/4620, while its previous registration mark, # 12203, still remains valid for tracing it.

Later on, all those crumbly and decrepit pages will undergo conservation at our laboratory in order to properly preserve the document for generations.

We greatly appreciate your important efforts and consideration.

Most sincerely,

M. Shraberman

Mark Shraberman
Acquisitions

---

81   The name Goldstein Hermanne is the way Bracha signed of her memoir in Hungarian. It translates as the wife of Herman Goldstein. This married synonym

Appendix B – Poems written by Holocaust Survivors.

These are poems written by holocaust survivors before and after liberation. These were poems kept by my mother that were given to her by other holocaust survivors. She kept them hidden along with her memoir.

As I was translating these poems[82], I could not help but feel the pain and suffering of these survivors. These poems evoke some extraordinarily strong emotions that could very easily be tearjerker. We can see many tears dropped on the original Hungarian copies.

These poems were most probably written after liberation, and they relate the conditions and feelings these inmates experienced during the Holocaust. Some of them also express the very strong human emotion of yearning for freedom and hope for the future.

One could ask why author poems about the horrors of Nazi terror?

---

name was used by Yad Vashem to file her historic memoir.

[82] The translation of these poems was done to assure that the meanings and the feelings expressed in the poems were preserved. As a result, an exact verbatim translation was not followed.

The rational mind could not comprehend the enormity of the crime committed against the Jewish civilians - men, women, and children. There was no logical way to explain any of the horrible German acts of hatred and sadistic pleasure in terrorizing and killing innocent people. Poetry was the one way that some of the victims were able to express their emotions, their feelings, their pain, and suffering as well as their yearning for freedom.

These poems prove that many of the Jewish people kept their humanity despite the German effort to dehumanize them. The persecuted Jewish people had the mental capacity and the humanity to be able to express their agonizingly painful feelings in beautifully crafted poetry.

Remembrance
1945 - month of Nisan- Beendorf

It would be good to be an animal instead of a man,
And only think of what we can eat next.
Not thinking of your parents or your brothers,
Not thinking of how we were last year together.

Sometimes I succeed to forget for a few days,
And I am looking for joy even in the bitterness.
Like getting a nice slice of bread or
Getting a nice potato instead of a rotten carrot.

But I am a man, a very broken man,
With agonizing bitter thoughts
The hellish pain now is stronger than me
The crying is shaking my shoulders
frozen to the bones.

I can see my father covered in snow white clothing,
With his hand holding a big seder plate
Giving us little packets with bitter herbs
We wait in line from his holy hand to take

"Manishtana" why is our people's fate,
So different from that of all the other people?
Why are we living on bitter herbs?
Why are we always living at the mercy of others?

My dear younger brother it has been more than a year,
Since I heard you ask the questions at the seder table.
I wish I could see your beautiful face.
With hellish desire I am longing for your embrace.

My dear wonderful mother, my holy father,
Helen my sister and all those at our table
Will I ever see you again?
Will I ever celebrate with you again?

The bitter reality is that my noble parent and siblings,
Will only be with me in my dreams.
Auschwitz's blind thick fog swallowed you,
Then what is the value of God's world without you?

Will I ever be able to ask forgiveness in my earthly life,
For what I might have done wrong to any of you?
My only holy prayer that I am asking from God,
Is to be able to kiss the ground that you stepped on.

To be able again to sit at a seder table,
With a golden chicken soup and matza balls
And be able to open the front door,
And together welcome Eliyahu Hanavi

Auschwitz - 1944

The skies of Auschwitz are burning red
from the flames,
The air is filled with smoke soot,
The Jewish lives are cheap and
worthless,
You hand out death, Mengele.

May 5, 1945 – Liberation

Your power is over – The clock has
struck.
The big showdown has come.
We lived to see this happen,
Our dreams have come true.

We will revenge our parents, siblings,
And all the other relatives
Who will never return.
But they will pay for this.

We were all in fear of you,
You were the angel of death.
You led the way in Auschwitz,
One goes one way to the left or to the
right.

You sent millions to the gas chambers,
They knew at the end what will happen
to them,
And whispering they said "Baruch atah
Adojnai"
(Blessed be our God)

You heroes, you saints on the wings of flames
You are now marching armies in heaven,
You will never come back again.
But they will pay for this.

My heart is full of grief and poison,
And I could not escape the Lord's hand.
But for the thousands of innocent children's blood
One death is not enough for you.

It will also be the turn of the slave drivers,
To be cut out from the civilized world
Who had a most vicious, cruel-hearted,
Animal-like behavior toward us.

My dearest father and mother you are up in heaven.
Please watch out for your orphaned children.
Ask our good Lord to give us the strength,
To be able to avenge you.

Past and the Present
(1945 at the Danish border)

Thousands of nights with rosy dreams
Are becoming real in our life,
Sentenced to death in a deep abyss,
God's miracle saved our lives.

Yesterday 100 deaths were searching for us.
Yesterday we were shaking the handcuffs on our hands.
But today a new dawn has sprung on our night,
Our jail door has been opened and soon we will be free.

Yesterday we were watching the cruel Nazis,
With our painful eyes and our withered hearts,
While outside life was blooming in full glory.

Today our eyes are sparkling from all that's happening.
Our head does not know if this is reality or just a dream.
Is it real that we are at the Danish border at the brink of freedom?

Many, many, wonderful Red Cross cars
With guards all around them
Are bringing delicious food bites,
To all the refugees surrounding them.

What an incredible feeling to leave the cattle wagons
Our miserable moving prison,
And get into a real passenger train,
With velvet covered seats.

This train is taking us faster and faster,
Through some marvelous sites toward freedom.
Say goodbye to the past, let's forget the bad
And all our thoughts are with a future life.

Appendix   C   -   Family Memorabilia

Bracha and Tzvi's postcards while they were dating.

Lady with a pet dog representing Loyalty.

Bracha with this postcard was reminding Tzvi of his promise of loyalty.

Handwritten in Hungarian

Loyalty and Amore (love)

Picture Postcard sent by Bracha to Tzvi on May 19, 1929 —

"Pleasant Goldstein,

Since I do not want my word to be misunderstood, this card
should be reminding you that with time passing you should
not forget me so easily.

Do not forget what we promised (each other in the middle
of) the flowering lilac (bushes).

With Memories from Boris (Bracha) "

She addresses him very formally as Mr. Goldstein.
The address is just the town Valea lui Mihai,

and the postcard was sent Local – meaning within the small town of Valea lui Mihai.

No street number or street name.
It seems that the local mailman knew where to find Herman (Tzvi) Goldstein.
Probably in the Goldstein Book Store.

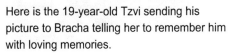

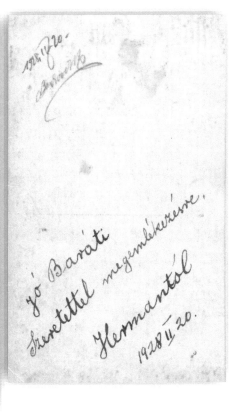

Here is the 19-year-old Tzvi sending his picture to Bracha telling her to remember him with loving memories.

With very friendly loving memories

From Herman (Tzvi)

March 20, 1928

The Wedding of Bracha to Tzvi (my parents) in 1935

Although most of the possessions of Hungarian Jews were looted or destroyed by their neighbors, when Jews were deported to German concentration camps, this surviving photograph of Bracha and Tzvi wedding was recovered since it had no intrinsic value to the neighbors.

I was able to identify the following people in the wedding photograph:

A.   Joszi Bauer – Bride's youngest brother
B.   Victor Bauer – Bride's father
C.   Shaindy Bauer – Bride's mother
D.   Bracha (Boris) Bauer – My mother, the bride
E.   Tzvi (Herman) Goldstein – My father, the Groom
F.   Frida Goldstein - Groom's youngest sister
G.   Moshe (Moric) Goldstein's first wife
H.   Miriam (Manci) Bauer – Bride's younger sister
I.   Max (Menyus) Goldstein's son with first wife Piroska.
J.   Piroska – Max Goldstein's first wife
K.   Julius (Gyula) Bauer – Bride's younger brother
L.   Rivka (Regina) Goldstein – Groom's sister
M. Moshe (Moric) Goldstein – Groom's brother
N.   Esther Goldstein – Groom's sister
O.   Max (Menyus) Goldstein – Groom's brother

The Wedding of Miriam and Baruch in 1947

The Wedding of Miriam and Baruch Rooz in 1947

I was able to identify the following people in the wedding party:

A. Bracha (Barbara) Goldstein – Bride's 35 years old sister
B. Miriam Bauer - The 31-year-old Bride
C. Baruch Rooz - The 40-year-old Groom
D. Tom Goldstein - 6-month-old author in his father's lap
E. Tzvi (Herman) Goldstein – Bride's 38-year-old brother-in-law (Bracha's husband)
F. Ilona Bauer – Bride's 26-year-old Sister-in-Law (Julius' wife)
G. Julius (Gyula) Bauer – Bride's 29-year-old Brother
H. Miklos Szobel – Newspaper Reporter – Family friend
I. Greti Lebovitz – Bride's first cousin who was with her in Sweden
J. Suri Bauer – Bandi Bauer's 27-year-old wife
K. Bandi Bauer – Bride's 28-year-old first cousin –
L. Manci Roth (Mati Manci) – Groom's sister –
M. Mati Roth – Groom's brother-in-law –
N. Laicsi Riez – Bride's relative
O. Frida (Goldstein) Fraifeld – Herman Goldstein's Sister

Anna Rooz and Jancu Leibel engagement of in 1963

I was able to identify the following people in the
engagement party:

A. Miriam Rooz (the bride's mother)
B. Ella Rooz (the bride's sister)
C. Anna Rooz (the bride)
D. Jancu Leibel (the groom)
E. Abraham Leibel (the groom's father)
F. Brocha (Barbara) Goldstein (Bride's aunt) author of the
   Hidden Memoir
G. Tzvi (Herman) Goldstein (Bride's uncle) Brocha's
   husband
H. Gizela Goldstein (Bride's once removed cousin)
I. Thomas Goldstein (bride's first cousin) author of this
   book

J. Adel Goldstein (Bride's once removed aunt)
K. Erica (distant relative)
L. Ilona Bauer (Bride's aunt)
M. Joseph Goldstein (Bride's first cousin) editor of this book
N. Ildiko Roth (Bride's First cousin)
O. Steve (Tibi) Bauer (Bride's first cousin)
P. Shalom Leibel (Groom's younger brother)

Family Trees

Family Trees

Bracha (Bauer) Goldstein's
Parents, Siblings with Spouses

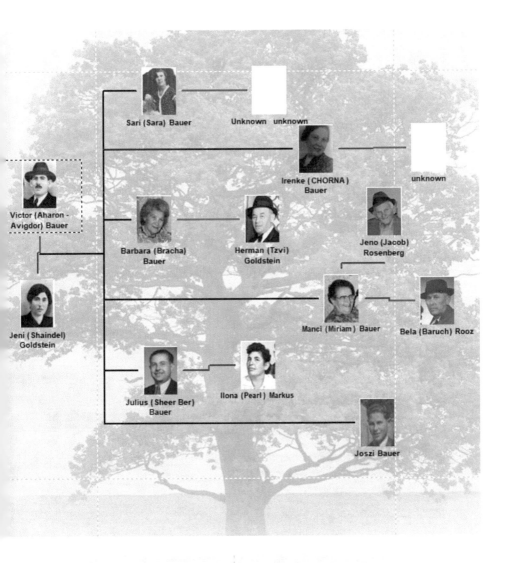

Tzvi Goldstein's Parents, Siblings with their Spouses

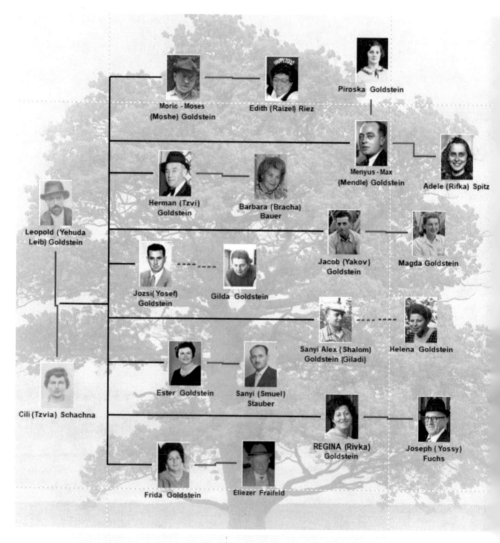

Piroska Goldstein

Moric - Moses (Moshe) Goldstein

Edith (Raizel) Riez

Menyus - Max (Mendle) Goldstein

Adele (Rifka) Spitz

Herman (Tzvi) Goldstein

Barbara (Bracha) Bauer

Leopold (Yehuda Leib) Goldstein

Jacob (Yakov) Goldstein

Magda Goldstein

Jozsi (Yosef) Goldstein

Gilda Goldstein

Sanyi Alex (Shalom) Goldstein (Giladi)

Helena Goldstein

Ester Goldstein

Sanyi (Smuel) Stauber

Cili (Tzvia) Schachna

REGINA (Rivka) Goldstein

Joseph (Yossy) Fuchs

Frida Goldstein

Eliezer Fraifeld

References - Sources of Knowledge

Satellite picture of the road built by the Jewish Slave Laborers

This satellite image displays the road constructed on the Carpathian Mountain ridge in Romania by the Jewish labor brigade. Notice the treacherous mountain ridges where they had to work. It is highly likely that many lost their lives during the harsh winter months while laboring on these mountain peaks.

These roads served as crucial routes for the Hungarian and German armies to traverse the mountains and access Russia. The satellite images reveal the incredibly winding nature of this road, which is still in use today for crossing the towering peaks of the Carpathian Alps

Nutrition in Auschwitz-Birkenau

(From the Auschwitz Museum archives)

Prisoners received three meals per day. In the morning, they received only half a liter of "coffee," or rather boiled water with a grain-based coffee substitute added, or "tea"—a herbal brew. These beverages were usually unsweetened. The noon meal consisted of about a liter of soup, the main ingredients of which were potatoes, rutabaga, and small amounts of groats, rye flour, and Avo food extract. The soup was unappetizing, and newly arrived prisoners were often unable to eat it or could do so only in disgust. Supper consisted of about 300 grams (10 ounces) of black bread, served with about 25 grams (0.9 ounces) of sausage, or margarine, or a tablespoon of marmalade or cheese. The bread served in the evening was supposed to cover the needs of the following morning as well, although the famished prisoners usually consumed the whole portion at once. The low nutritional value of these meals should be noted.

The combination of insufficient nutrition and hard labor contributed to the destruction of the organism, which gradually used up its stores of fat, muscle mass, and the tissues of the internal organs. This led to emaciation and starvation sickness, the cause of a significant number of deaths in the camp. A prisoner suffering from starvation sickness was referred to as a "Mussulman," and could easily fall victim to selection for the gas chambers.

Historical Facts Regarding Nazi Underground Factories

Last Secrets of Nazi Terror—An Underground Labor Camp

The Guardian. October 25, 2005.

Last Secrets of Nazi Terror—an Underground Labor Camp | Encyclopedia.com

https://www.encyclopedia.com/history/legal-and-political-magazines/last-secrets-nazi-terror-underground-labor-camp

Underground Nazi weapon factory discovered by the Allies.

Underground Nazi weapon factory discovered by the Allies was one of the most extraordinary finds of World War II | The Vintage News

https://www.thevintagenews.com/2016/09/29/underground-nazi-weapon-factory-discovered-allies-one-extraordinary-finds-world-war-ii/

Cyprus Detention Camps

(from United State Holocaust Memorial Museum)

https://encyclopedia.ushmm.org/cont
ent/en/article/cyprus-detention-camps

Between Aug 1946 to May 1948, the British Navy intercepted more than 50,000 Holocaust survivors seeking to reach British mandate of Palestine. The British interned these people in the detention camps on the island of Cyprus in the middle of the Mediterranean Sea.

Population of the Camps

In all, the British detained about 52,000 *ma'apilim* (illegal immigrants) in Cyprus, including about 1,300 from North Africa. The Cyprus detainees were primarily young people who had joined Zionist youth groups before departing Europe. Approximately 80 percent were aged 12 to 35, while 8,000 were between the ages of 12 and 18. The majority were orphans.

Conditions in the Camps

The British military ran the detention camps in accordance with the harsh model of the POW camp. Surrounded by barbed wire and watch towers, the camps were under constant guard. The Joint Distribution Committee provided for the welfare of the detainees, including supplying food and medical care, mitigating the hardships suffered by the detainees.

Conditions were generally harsh. People were squeezed into tents and tin huts that were unbearably hot in the summer and freezing cold in the rainy winter, with little furniture, no electric lighting, limited access to water, bad food, and poor sanitary conditions.

Approximately 2000 babies were born in the Cyprus camps. The births took place in the Jewish wing of the British military hospital in Nicosia. Four hundred Jews died during their internment on the island and were buried in the Margoa cemetery.

The British were successful in apprehending most of the 70,000 illegal immigrants who embarked for Palestine. Nonetheless, as space for refugees on Cyprus became scarce and ships continued to sail from Europe carrying *ma'apilim*, it became apparent to the British that the policy of detention in Cyprus was not successful in deterring the *Ha'apala* movement. The conditions in the Cyprus detentions camps and the sight of Jewish Holocaust survivors being held behind barbed wire also excited widespread criticism of British handling of the problem of Jewish immigration to Palestine. The British decision to send the refugee ship *Exodus 1947* back to Europe in July 1947 instead of detaining its passengers on

Cyprus represented an admission of the failure of the Cyprus deterrent.

For most of those survivors interned in Cyprus, the experience only served to strengthen their resolve to reach Palestine, which they almost all did following the creation of Israel in May 1948.

Oradea Ghetto (from en.wikipedia.org)

Oradea Ghetto
https://en.wikipedia.org/wiki/Oradea_ghetto#p-search

The **Oradea ghetto** was one of the Nazi-era ghettos for European Jews during World War II. It was located in the city of Oradea (Hungarian: *Nagyvárad*) in Bihor County, Transylvania, now part of Romania but administered as part of Bihar County by the Kingdom of Hungary from the 1940 Second Vienna Award's grant of Northern Transylvania until late 1944. The ghetto was active in the spring of 1944 following Operation Margarethe

History

Aside from the Budapest ghetto, this was the largest ghetto in Hungary. There were in fact two ghettos in the city. The first, for Oradea's Jews, numbered 27,000 inhabitants and was situated near the Orthodox synagogue and the Great Square. The second contained nearly 8,000 Jews from the many rural communities of a dozen districts: Aleșd, Berettyóújfalu, Biharkeresztes, Cefa, Derecske, Marghita, Oradea, Săcueni, Sălard, Salonta, Sárrétudvari and Vale a lui Mihai. Many Jews from these communities were also placed around the Mezey lumber yard.[1]

The ghetto was strikingly overpopulated. The Oradea Jews, who formed 30% of the city's population, were crowded into an area sufficient for one-fifteenth of the city. Conditions were such that one room had to shelter fourteen or fifteen Jews. As in other ghettoes, Oradea's suffered from a lack of food and drink. The local authorities, unusually vehement in their anti-Semitism, created victims with their punitive measures. They often interrupted the flow of electricity and water to the ghetto. Furthermore, the gendarmes, commanded by lieutenant-colonel Jenő Péterffy, were especially sadistic in their searches for valuables, which took place right by the ghetto in the Dréher brewery. Internal administration took place under the auspices of a Judenrat headed by Sándor Leitner, leader of the local Orthodox Jewish community.[1] In the spring of 1944 the ghetto was evacuated in nine transports, the first two from the lumber yard and the remainder from the city: May 23 (3,110), May 25 (3,148), May 28 (3,227), May 29 (3,166), May 30 (3,187), June 1 (3,059), June 3 (2,972), June 5 (2,527), June 27 (2,819). Thus, with 6,258 Jews in the first category and 20,957 in the second, a total of 27,215 Jews were sent to the Auschwitz concentration camp.[1][2]

The June 27 transport involved Jews from the part of Bihar County that remained in Hungary following the Treaty of Trianon. Coming from small communities south and southeast of Debrecen, such as Derecske and Konyár, they were brought to Oradea on June 16–17.[3] Thus, while the ghetto was originally part of the Cluj military district,[4] it was transferred to the Debrecen district during the period when this last group of deportees lived there.[5]

Jewish History of Hungary and Romania

Valea lui Mihai (Érmihályfalva), Romania KehilaLink (jewishgen.org)	https://kehilalinks.jewishgen.org/valea_lui_mihai/
Category:Jewish Romanian history - Wikipedia	https://en.wikipedia.org/wiki/Category:Jewish_Romanian_history
Category:Jewish Hungarian history - Wikipedia	https://en.wikipedia.org/wiki/Category:Jewish_Hungarian_history
Category:Jewish ghettos in Nazi-occupied Hungary - Wikipedia	https://en.wikipedia.org/wiki/Category:Jewish_ghettos_in_Nazi-occupied_Hungary

Category:1944 establishments in Hungary - Wikipedia	https://en.wikipedia.org/wiki/Category:1944_establishments_in_Hungary

Acknowledgements

To My Dearest Wife, Judy

Your willingness to dive into the pages of this book and offer your honest insightful review has touched me profoundly. I know how difficult it is for you to read or talk about the Holocaust which you experienced through your own mother's and father's terrifying history.

As I embark on this literary journey to preserve my mother's memory, I thank you for all your help and for being the compass that guides me through the labyrinth of life. You are my life partner, my confidante, my inspiration, and my friend whom I love dearly.

Rabbi Yaakov Luban

We extend our heartfelt gratitude to Rabbi Luban for his decades-long friendship, guidance, and unwavering dedication to our community. His kind words and steadfast support hold profound significance for us, and we are truly honored to feature his endorsement in our book.

Rabbi Luban served as the Executive Rabbinic Coordinator at the Orthodox Union and currently holds the esteemed position of Rabbi Emeritus at Congregation Ohr Torah in Edison, NJ. He is also a respected member of the Va'ad HaRabbonim of Raritan Valley. Additionally, Rabbi Luban has authored numerous articles in prominent journals and magazines. He has curated a substantial collection of inspiring shiurim available online that emphasize treating others with dignity as well as the values of midot, chesed, and Torah study.

Rabbi Bernhard Rosenberg

Many thanks to our neighbor and friend Rabbi Rosenberg, for his invaluable insights and guidance in assisting with this publication. We deeply appreciate his extensive years of dedication to the community and the warmth of his friendship towards our family.

Rabbi Rosenberg is renowned radio and television personality, as well as an accomplished author with numerous publications on Holocaust history to his credit. His significant contributions extend to his role as the Chairman of New Jersey State Holocaust Commission, where he played a pivotal role in the introduction of Holocaust history studies in NJ Public High Schools. He is also the recipient of the Dr. Martin Luther King Jr Humanitarian Award.

Rabbi Yaakov Tesser

Our sincere appreciation to Rabbi Tesser for his generous words and support of this publication. We are thankful for his enduring friendship and his tireless, dynamic efforts in serving the Aberdeen community.

Rabbi Tesser holds the esteemed position of Mara d'Atra at the Young Israel of Aberdeen - Congregation Bet Tefilah, where he has cultivated a warm and vibrant community, offering numerous programs for individuals of all ages. Additionally, he is the founder of the community Kollel and is known as an educator who effectively connects with all students at various levels.

Lynda and Dr. David Trutt

I am immensely grateful to our dear friends and former neighbors, Lynda and David, for their exceptional support in reviewing and refining this book. Lynda, with her background as a technical writer, brings a meticulous attention to detail and a mastery of language that greatly enhanced the quality of this work. Her dedication and expertise were evident in every aspect of the review process, ensuring the accuracy and clarity of the book.

I deeply value the time and effort they both dedicated to meticulously examining each section, and I sincerely thank you for generously sharing your knowledge and expertise with me.

Dr. Jeffrey Galler

I extend thanks to Dr. Jeffrey Galler, who has been our steadfast friend and parenting partner throughout our years together. Jeffrey, in addition to being a highly regarded dentist, also excels as a newspaper columnist and a medical journal editor.

His invaluable input in refining the style, content, structure, and syntax of this book is deeply appreciated. We are very lucky to have him as our family partner and friend.

Yossi Pollak

I extend my heartfelt gratitude to my beloved brother-in-law, Yossi Pollak, for his generous investment of time, invaluable advice, and guidance throughout the review of this book. Additionally, I want to express my appreciation for his unwavering love and support over the years, strengthening the bond of our close-knit family.

Joseph Goldstein

My dear brother Joe Goldstein deserves special thanks for his pivotal role in preserving our mother's memoir. Joe's initiative in locating the memoir and arranging for its donation to Yad Vashem in Jerusalem, Israel, ensures that this valuable document will be safeguarded in their climate-controlled historical archive.

Furthermore, Joe's vivid memories and detailed recollections of our mother greatly enriched the content of this publication. I am deeply grateful for his contribution in this regard.

Beyond his contributions to this project, I want to express my appreciation for Joe's unwavering support and companionship. Whether during moments of joy or times of adversity, Joe has consistently been a pillar of strength and reliability. His presence in my life as a true brother is a source of immense comfort and gratitude. I feel truly blessed to have such a remarkable and close brother.

Gisela Axelrod

I express my gratitude to my beloved cousin, Gisela, whose expertise as a language teacher greatly contributed to the improvement of this book. Gisela's insightful revisions have enhanced the logical organization and readability of the text, making it more accessible to readers. Additionally, I appreciate Gisela's dedication to reviewing and documenting our extended family history during our invaluable sessions together. Her efforts have added depth and richness to our collective story.

Made in the USA
Columbia, SC
21 July 2024